Surviving The Human Zoo

Anthony Asquith Dip Hyp Psych UK

The game changing book on stress management, coping with anxiety and thinking positive in the twenty first century...

This book will help you relax more, worry less and be happier

About the Author

Anthony Asquith is a solution focused psychotherapist who qualified in 2000 and has a keen interest in human behaviour.

Anthony has worked since 2004 with thousands of NHS staff across the UK on courses ranging from personality profiling, managing complaints, handling stress, managing change, nudge technique and working with strong personality types.

His NHS work is with Dentcom Training and you can visit his website **www.dentcomtraining.co.uk**

You can also visit his D.I.S.C. Human Behaviour Workshop site at **www.affinitytraining.org** where you can get details on his pioneering work helping individuals have more success in their personal relationships

If you would like to receive the 'Better Connected' monthly newsletter too then please feel free to leave your email address details at either web site

If you wish to correspond with Anthony please do feel free to get in touch by email at **anthonyasquith@ntlworld.com** or you can read regular blogs at **http://www.dentcomtraining.co.uk/blogs.html**

Contents

Special offer to you...

Thanks for choosing to purchase this book, I am grateful for your interest in my ideas and would like by way of a thank you to offer you additional material which is exclusive to people like you who choose to buy my book and join my soft skills revolution.

Visit my home page at www.affinitytraining.org and type in your name and email address into the red collection box.

You will receive a copy of my white paper entitled 'Negotiation Greats' which examines the latest psychology of negotiating and how to help others be more flexible to your ideas and more often will help you reach a win/win situation. It's packed with great insights and aha moments.

You will additionally receive regular newsletters and video feeds on fantastic stuff all about being human ranging from the latest ideas on nudge technique right through spotting if people are being deceitful or telling you the honest truth.www.affinitytraining.org

Managing stress and surviving the human zoo

Are you struggling to relax, remain calm, perhaps having problems sleeping due to worry or feeling like the world conspires against you? Guess what, that's what it is to be human. In the UK it's been reported that Britons spend around 2 hours a day worrying about their health, finances, weight and wellbeing of their kids plus a whole host of other things. That's around 5 years in a lifetime and in other parts of the western world some spend up to 6.5 years with women being significantly more susceptible to worry than men.

I have a simple message which is that you aren't weak willed, going mad, or a lesser person than anyone else because of these things. If you are like millions of other people, you'll be experiencing malaise, self-medicating on alcohol, porn, pain killers, shopping, anti-depressants, over eating or taking recreational drugs to relax. The worries, fears and issues you fight with every day are what it is to be human in the digital age. Where you are right now is what it is to be surviving and just getting by in the human zoo. This book will show you how to thrive instead.

Our brains, as I will reveal, aren't yet evolved to cope so well yet with the pace of change in the 21st century and all that this brings. So here's a starting point for you!

'So long as you have a pulse, are awake, breathing and conscious with blood flowing in your veins, there's probably a lot more right about you than there is wrong.'

These fears, issues and inabilities are the condition of 'Human Beings'. Not only that, we have gone from human beings and are rapidly becoming 'Human Doings'. Our western culture encourages us to do more, consume stuff, work harder, be better, thrive and look good in front of others. These are just constructs put upon us by conditioning from advertisers, the media, education and outmoded historical cultural values that for many, no longer serve a useful purpose.

As a psychotherapist who's been working with thousands of people in the last 15 years, I see the massive volumes of advertising and wonder if people are being hypnotised into buying trances which require them to buy things like the latest designer gear, the best cars, the latest smart phones or a bigger house in order for their lives to feel valid or worthwhile.

'This is just shit brained thinking!'

Terence McKenna- Philosopher 'Reclaim Your Mind'

None of it will make you happier, for any long period, no more than maybe just a couple of weeks…end of!!! I'll explain why in this book too. That said however, there is much you can do in order to make your existence a lot happier without succumbing to the commercialised, consumerist programming that is being thrown at you every day and furthermore this book has many, many interesting insights into how to see the world around you for what it is and some easy to use tips to help complement your existing skills in mind management in the high speed 21st century world. I sincerely hope you will find a compelling read.

Why are we in the human zoo?

The scientific community believes the universe formed 13.5 billion years ago and earth came into existence around 3 billion years ago. Monkeys evolved along with other mammals after the end of the dinosaurs, approximately 165 million years ago. Modern man appeared around 200,000 years back and we developed our unique and very wonderful modern logical brain or frontal region, around 20,000 years ago which suggests that it's very new. It's rather like the new kid on the block and has to get used to a new place, new friends and all the struggles of being the new kid.

To give you a sense of timescale about just how new man and the modern brain fits in, take a 12 month calendar and allocate the entire history of the universe from January to December. Each day in the calendar would be a period equivalent to around 40 million years.

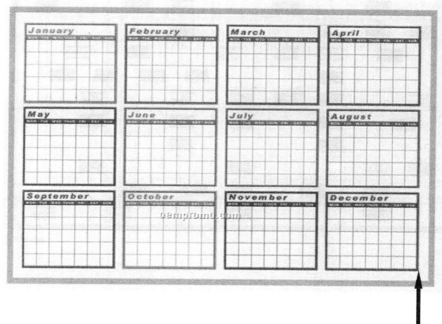

Modern Man Appears Here!!!

Man has existed since the beginning of the very last day of this calendar and clocked in at around 6.00pm.

The modern logical brain (frontal region) appears about 11.59pm. Which means the 20,000 years since the frontal region developed would be the equivalent of a few seconds before midnight on the very last day of the calendar. This newer logical frontal area of the brain is literally just like I said, the new kid on the block.

Prior to the modern brain we had other brain structures which helped or perhaps also hindered our existence! One region is known as the lizard brain... however I will refer to this limbic system as the 'Ape' region to avoid confusing myself!! Here is an easy example to show you where these are situated in the brain's schematics. Although it's not anatomically exact, it'll give you basic reference points for understanding the structures in play.

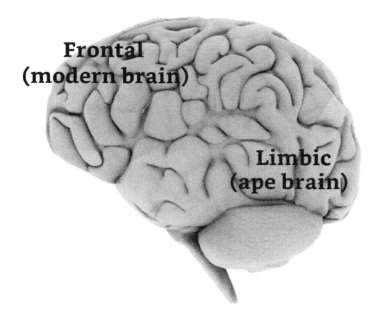

We have a brain in our head that's been around a while now but change within it takes an entire lifetime and the modern brain is very much in its infancy as it really only fully developed around 20,000 years ago. The continuing development of this modern brain, I would argue, has however not kept up with the pace and speed of scientific development we've seen in the last 25 years.

To illustrate my point, cast your mind back to the earliest mobile phone bricks - which you yourself may have carried round with a charge pack - weighing in at several pounds. Compare them with the modern day smart phone which is now tiny in comparison, one hell of a lot faster and you can do a lot more with it too. Yet our brain and its structure, size and shape, if you were alive back then, is pretty much unchanged! We can send people into space, we can split the atom, we've discovered numerous cures for diseases, built buildings that are extraordinarily complex and now use pilotless aircraft for a whole range of things and yet, we can't manage our overwhelming emotions, stress disorders, depression or anxiety.

Which suggests that it (the brain), isn't currently a great body for change and there's more, a whole lot more. In his book, The Chimp Paradox, Dr Steve Peters describes the limbic brain as the 'Chimp' mind and the frontal region as the human mind. He then explains that a chimp is around 5 times stronger than a man and in a fight will almost always win.

The real trick about this stuff is to keep in mind that the more both parts of the brain can work in harmony or balance, the better your quality of thinking tends to be. To examine this, consider the fact that you get stimulus through your 5 senses. The information is immediately filtered through the limbic system, which describes the saying 'An emotional reaction'. This is then made sense of logically by the more modern brain and provided these two work together in harmony, both run the human really, really well.

So we have a prehistoric 'Ape' mind that sometimes inappropriately out-muscles our logical human brain; trouble is though, the Ape mind applies strategies that were useful several million years back but often aren't so clever in the modern digital age. Is it any wonder that people relate to the idea that they're living in the human zoo?

Session 1

Getting to grips with your thinking

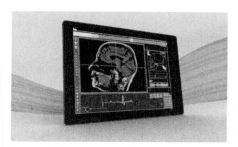 Neuroscientists are turning to FMRI (Functional Magnetic Resonance Imaging) technology which opens up so many possibilities in neuro science. It allows us to watch and examine blood flow inside the brain of live subjects as well as oxygenation and brain temperature, which identify which parts of the brain switch on and off when exposed to different stimuli and inputs.

The mind seeks reward and avoids threats

Think about the last time you were given a pay rise, bought a new outfit or shoes or maybe a newer, smarter car than the one you drove previously. How about the last time you had sex or saw another person who aroused you sexually, maybe you had a wonderful date last night or succeeded in getting a job or promotion recently. Perhaps you have done something minor and mundane like eaten chocolate recently, won a bet at the bookies or you had a hunch about someone or a situation that turned out to be right! These are all experiences that are associated with rewards and when we get these, something interesting happens in our brain. We get a small dose of endorphins such as Oxytocin which is a brain neurotransmitter associated with the pleasure of feeling connected or maybe dopamine which our brain produces during situations that create curiosity or excitement.

Experiments done by Keise Izuma in 2008 demonstrated that subjects who heard a robotic voice telling them they'd done a 'Good job' had their brain regions light up under FMRI scanning in the same region as the reward area in the brain linked to receiving a financial windfall.

That said though, how long is it before we're left thinking again that there's too much month still left at the end of the money? The newer smarter car you've been driving around in and enjoying has been bashed in a local car park, has picked up some minor dents and is dirty more often as you don't have the time to wash it every week and you've gone from this being an experience to be enjoyed to a motor car that just gets us from A to B. The new romantic interest is a damp squib because they no longer return your calls, the promotion and role isn't working out or you're a parent who's exhausted by sleepless nights because the baby simply won't settle and worse still, you've eaten all the chocolate and feel bloated and give yourself a hard time thereafter. Doesn't this sound all too familiar?

That's all due to the fact that the brain likes a reward but these don't hold our attention for long periods. Our 'Ape' brains tend to pay more attention to the threats, real or imagined, that we face than the potential of rewards. Not only that, the threats that we feel hit us faster and quicker, they hold our attention for longer periods, they make our emotions deeper and darker and physiologically hit us sometimes like a bullet train which comes out of nowhere, all courtesy of the 'Ape' mind muscling in over the logical human brain. I heard Dr Srini Pillay MD of Harvard University talk about this and he gave an amazing example of experiments done where children were observed throwing a toy out of its cot and then crying loudly. At this point the mother would pick it up and bring it back to the baby who'd stop crying, smile for a few minutes and then repeatedly throw the toy out only to begin crying again whilst the mother fetched it back. He suggested that we could see this in later life where adults now fully developed do something similar due to conditioning where they become more interested in handling and overcoming adversity than focusing on the possibility of the great things they could achieve. Rather like the way you have a project that doesn't go according to plan, if it fails you may react by saying that didn't go well but at least I handled the set back well. In other words despite the setback I was at least good at handling something. Here's a quick 20 second exercise to demonstrate in what way threats catch our attention…

What's this? ●

You'd be just about right saying that it is a black dot. Or would you? You'd be even more accurate in saying it's a black dot on a page in your book, or on your kindle app, on an iPad or smart phone which is in your hand or on the screen of your laptop. You may be sitting down in an office or café, lying down in bed or in the bath, perhaps standing in a queue, waiting to meet friends, on the bus, in the library, which is situated in a busy street, one of many in the small town or bigger city, you live somewhere in the UK, Europe or maybe you're overseas somewhere by a swimming pool.

What I am getting at is the fact that when faced with a threat, real or perceived, our Ape brain tends to focus down onto the immediate issue to be handled and we ignore all or most other stimuli.

This ability to focus our attention is run by our Ape brain region and allows us to act quickly because the frontal portion or logical brain takes too long to consider and philosophise over the situation. Which lead us to jump to conclusions, some of which aren't always correct, before we've had time to assimilate all the pertinent detail. Of course negative emotions are warnings for us to take action but in the human zoo things can go a little more than crazy!

We're turning into the worried well

Google UK searches over the past decade found that since the start of the recession in 2008 there has been a huge surge in people looking for terms related to their personal health. (Times Newspaper April 5th 2014)

Whilst there has been a long established link to stress, financial hardship and illness, the data also suggests that having experienced a financial crash, this can make us more susceptible to becoming anxious, hypochondriac and possibly worse, completely neurotic.

Times Newspapers' Data team recorded 13.5% more searches for health related terms than expected from pre-2008 trends accounting for more than 5 million extra searches and because the data is analysed as a proportion of existing searches, these findings simply don't reflect the increased numbers of people making use of the internet.

According to figures from the Health and Safety Executive, workplace stress costs Great Britain around £6bn and the numbers of workers seeking medical advice about stress rose by 110,0000 to 530,0000.

Britain lost around 14 million working days last year due to stress related illness and amazingly here in the UK, around 44,000 national health service staff call in sick every day!!

So what's the deal really?

Think about the last time you met someone new for the first time and were introduced or introduced yourself, they probably greeted you enthusiastically if you were friendly and smiled but then, within 45 seconds unless you have a recall strategy, you'd lost their name to your immediate memory and whilst continuing to smile and engage them, began to look for hints or tips about their true identity. What just happened? You actually had a very low level fight or flight response which caused the thalamus (a part of the limbic region) to go a bit off kilter. Hardly surprising that you can't then remember their name when this part of the brain has associations to memory recall! What is happening here is the limbic region or 'Ape brain' has taken over and it looks for cues and signals in the interaction to match previous pattern-matched experiences to assess you as a friend or foe. This scanning for danger takes place at a level beneath conscious awareness pretty much all the time.

It interprets things like voice tone, body language, gestures and micro-expressions to check out how friendly you appear. Ever notice how most people in the street appear indifferent? It's not that they don't care about you, it's that they care more about not being stressed out about unexpected hostility and use the strategy of appearing disinterested or reserved to protect themselves.

If you want to get someone speaking to you and have them feel comfortable quickly, the key requirement is for you to smile warmly and raise your eyebrows with the briefest of flashes. This will automatically make you appear approachable and friendly because it lowers people's automatic fight or flight response orientation, therefore they feel more at ease as they're less likely to be secreting noradrenaline or cortisol into their blood supply and more likely to have small secretions of oxytocin promoted by curiosity and relatedness as they get to know you better.

What do humans need in order to thrive?

I'd like to run you through some basic housekeeping which is really quick and easy to get your head around; I'll refer to this again later in the section.

In the world of Neuro Linguistic Programming (NLP) there is a presupposition introduced by Albert Korzybski in 1933 which is that 'the map is not the territory'. Nothing affects our perceptions more than one simple, easy to understand system which I have heard called the 'HALTS' index (you'll discover I am a great lover of acronyms).

HALTS stands for feeling that you are any of the following; Hungry, Angry, Late, Tired or Stressed. It's a simple self-assessment strategy that you can do anywhere by just stopping and noticing your mood and feelings.

If you're experiencing one or more of these HALTS feelings, your view of events will be affected and you may well get yourself into trouble with someone in your life or some organisation who's providing a service to you. This may result in you making a complaint just because your view of the map was out of kilter and you were less emotionally resilient.

Try keeping a mood diary for the next seven days. You'll notice that you're happier than you might imagine and moments of sadness are relatively short lived. You'll see that happiness moments are often linked to small things like a shared meeting with a friend, a nice visit to the café or a park, something relatively insignificant and often without major financial outlay.

The HALTS index deals with the most immediate physical requirements but there are other needs that are imperative to living life successfully. There's also a good number of needs' models which range from Abraham Maslow's Hierarchy of Needs to the popular Human Givens Model from the European Therapy Studies Institute to name but two.

The one I find most useful (only in terms of getting my own ideas across) is the model outlined by Australian business/neuroscience coach David Rock, entitled **'SCARF'** which is an acronym for the human needs: <u>S</u>tatus, <u>C</u>ertainty, <u>A</u>utonomy, <u>R</u>elatedness and <u>F</u>airness. These are like the HALTS index, almost always linked and have to be attended to in order for human beings to function well.

He raises the idea in his literature that the Human Brain is a social device which is closely linked to associations with other people. I agree with this but maybe you should try it on for size, after all, you are your own best scientist.

Consider this point for a moment or two.

If you're not involved with a task or absorbed in thinking about a task you're doing or about to do, you're likely to be thinking about yourself or someone else.

Does that feel about right for you? Most people from what I have seen, give a positive response to this, what do you think? What I am getting at is that our social needs are, from a brain function perspective, as important as any of the other basic needs commonly associated with good living.

How are human needs met?

Status

When dealing with others in our lives, our ape or limbic system is scanning for environmental cues for a happy and safe existence (often we're completely unaware of this going on), to establish if our relationship will be a fair trade of energy and status. If equality of status is occurring, we tend to find that our ape brain/limbic system will remain fairly calm during an interaction. Ongoing research by Professor Michael Marmott of University College London, along with his team, has for over 40 years, been running the Whitehall Study and this has established that there is a direct link to good health and wellbeing where workers perceive themselves to have status and authority in their workplace compared to those who work in lower order occupations within the UK government. What actually constitutes status requirements being met will depend on individual situations and the people involved - that said, if the individual perceives there is status inequality against them then, according to research from Kidehio Takahashi et al in 2009, they can experience a fight or flight response. This seems to suggest that we have biological programming that associates our status because it seems to favour our survival too!

So let me give you an example of this.

Imagine you go to meet a business acquaintance and they run late without arranging to call and let you know they're on their way - it's possible that you might feel a little unhappy because they hadn't been considerate in calling you. You have a busy life too! Perhaps there's even a little 'HALTS' activity firing off within you. You decide to wait and when they do arrive, they apologise for keeping you waiting but as this isn't the first time and their apology is a bit half hearted, this makes you feel uncomfortable because even at this point, your sensitivity button about status may have been pushed and your Ape brain is now searching for additional evidence. You are then joined by another colleague in the meeting only to find your first colleague makes a dismissive comment about your ideas about the business you're discussing and now you're beginning to have a much stronger internalised reaction. You then add your opinion, with the best possible intentions and they question the thought process you had in an overly suspicious way, as well as asking for independent verification. In your mind now, you're frustrated and can feel the heat rising out of your collar! This is like being under attack and sounds all too familiar - even if the circumstances I just described aren't what you currently experience, there is a myriad of similar situations occurring in your life that are reminiscent.

Loss of status can occur in many possible areas of life. Write one or two brief notes by way of example of when this loss of status has happened to you and what you'll do the next time something like this happens.

I experienced a loss of status when XYZ occurred and when this happens again, I will do XYZ to avoid getting disappointed.

_____

_____

_____

Certainty

Researchers now know that human beings crave certainty because feeling unsure or vulnerable to the possibility of not knowing what can happen next leaves some humans anxious or worse debilitated.

Reuters the news agency reported in March 2014 that there were 32 million cars registered in 2013!! Breath taking to consider the volume of traffic these days and this is a record. Frankly I had no idea the numbers were so high. It still amazes me though with so many cars on the road - and the original rules were conceived in the 1930s - that we don't see a whole lot more car accidents occurring than actually do. The Office of National Statistics reported that there were around 147,000 accidents reported to the police in 2013. The road traffic act planners of 1930 couldn't have foretold the huge popularity of the motor vehicle.

The act of driving for most of us is something we can do quite easily, the more experienced you become, the more you can do this almost in an automatic way. How many times have you driven somewhere and actually couldn't recall most of the journey? It would seem that the brain will naturally conserve your attention and energy by utilising pattern-matched associations around driving to do this easily, whilst you think about something completely different in your mind. That said, the car in front suddenly brakes sharply and you jam on the brakes just stopping a few feet short. I am sure you'd agree that this or any other similar incident would be un-nerving! Funnily enough

16

thereafter, your mind is playing tricks then because you're thinking, 'That was close, good job I was vigilant and read the situation well enough, might be better to set off earlier tomorrow to avoid the heavy traffic.'

Of course the fight or flight system will have been triggered as a result of this and uncertainty will register in a region of the brain called the anterior cingulate cortex which lies deep in the limbic 'Ape' region of the brain and it may be sometime later in the day before you feel comfortable again.

Of course people who thrive in any walk of life have developed strategies for tolerating uncertainty better than others and rather than thinking, 'I don't know what to do next', they will begin to become mildly curious about the situation. The production of noradrenaline and cortisol, when in the correct mental context, i.e. 'This is new and I am excited and curious', can be a real boost to performance. You'll find in the work place or any other walk of life for that matter, there will be areas of uncertainty because you don't know what's around the corner these days. Will your company be downsizing, asking you to take a pay cut? Maybe they're introducing changes in working conditions? How will the economy perform, what about the mortgage or interest rates in the next 12 months and your own pension investments or personal health? These are all fairly typical uncertainties and you can record a few of your own in the table below.

Uncertainties I am facing now include XYZ and in the future I will deal with them by doing XYZ

_____

_____

_____

Autonomy

One major factor in the Whitehall study that impacted the health of individuals in the departments involved was their perception of control of their environment. This has also been seen in other animals too, like research by Steven Maier at Boulder University who established that the degree of control that the animal experienced in a stressful situation determined whether or not the stressor undermined its ability to function successfully. In any organisation or situation, provided a person feels they have some form of control, i.e. they are able to execute decisions or actions without too much micromanagement, stress in them can be controlled and managed. Humans are attuned to be aware of stressors, even at a subconscious level and a perception of being micro-managed can generate a threat response instantly which reduces their capacity to respond productively.

Any business or organisation which presents people with options and choices and sufficient latitude to make important business decisions, organise their working patterns and even set their own hours, can help provoke a greatly reduced stress response than forcing them under strict working rules and regulations. This is applicable to all organisations, employees and customers as indicated by research in 1977. Ellen Langer and Judith Rodin showed that residents in a care home who'd been given greater control in simple things such as meal menu choices, rather than having everything pre-selected for them, lived longer and felt healthier than those who weren't offered these choices. As I mentioned earlier, my work in the National Health Service has shown that increasingly, dental professionals are being subjected to greater legislation and compliance pressures. In the words of one BDA President, this was described as one of the worst times in history to come into UK dentistry and unfortunately, despite all this overwhelming evidence to show how rules can suck the life out of a work force, the drive for top down management, where the subservient workers remain unable to control many things in their workforce, continues unabated.

List one or two examples where your autonomy has been undermined by other people or organisations and what you might do to avoid this overwhelming you next time;

_____

_____

_____

Relatedness

I explained earlier that we feel a low level unconscious threat response when meeting others and our mind searches for cues that will reduce this initially, so will go into looking at things where there is a sense of connection between you and another person. These links can be surprisingly minor, such as sharing the same name, coming from the same part of the country as you do, having friends in common, doing a similar type of job, having an experience such as a holiday destination which you both have been to and are all subliminally a representation of your brain seeking evidence to confirm that this person poses no real threat to your own existence. Then it's safe to continue dealing with them, therefore reducing the fight flight or freeze responses in you.

If you're someone who runs a team in business, it's vital to know and use this to your best advantage because throwing a group of diverse people together where little or no relatedness occurs, will certainly be a majorly stressful event. Trust, goodwill and empathy need time to develop in working relationships and are a bi-product of when the brain begins to recognise former strangers as friends.

Examples of relatedness being undermined occur when a company's management team introduces system changes where insufficient consultation has taken place with those who are actually working there. This leads to ill will and the newly introduced system can fall foul due to resistance as a result of this. Again we now know that when relatedness occurs, oxytocin is produced and has been shown in 2005 when researched by Michael Kosfeld et al, to have a very positive effect on reducing the perceived threat response in people when delivered by something as unusual as a nasal spray. Much in the same way a shared joke, story or observation between people can achieve the same result.

Conversely the perception of being isolated is also a great stress response inducer and has been shown to produce arousal that is considered highly stressful too. This has been termed 'the science of loneliness'. In the US in 2010, around one in three adults reported feeling chronically lonely. The BBC news magazine reports that not only does loneliness affect one's health, it has been linked to many killing sprees undertaken where the teenage participants were considered to be loners too. This shows that loneliness isn't just linked to old age and bereavement, there is a distinct possibility that being lonely is a part of the busy lives we lead today, despite all the modern technologies that exist for us to collaborate.

Give examples of when you have experienced relatedness with others and also times when you have felt far removed from another and how that felt too! More importantly make a note to yourself about what you'll do when it happens again. Remember it's a temptation to just keep reading but time spent just making a note and thinking this stuff through will make a big difference as to how you might choose to react to this later when it occurs again.

Fairness

I believe this is one of the most important areas that effects everyone in so many ways. It's not just humans though, that feel the need for fairness, interestingly too is the fact that monkeys demand fairness. Visit youtube.com and type in Brainiac Cheating Monkey which shows what happens when a monkey is being cheated on during a card game.

If you have children or know friends with children you will know how the key to a happy existence with them is that you are fair to each of them and always notice when a friend or relative comes to visit you, insist that they each get a present or gift that holds equal value because failure to do so will almost always result in a total breakdown of harmony in an instant.

When dealing with other people or organisations in any walk of life, we need to feel that we have been treated fairly by others because if this doesn't happen, all hell can break loose. Again this is something driven from the limbic or old brain region. We've had a lot of controversy since 2008, following the breakdown of the financial systems around many countries in the Western World and whilst we were all enjoying prosperity there was no problem in our minds about bankers earning very high commissions etc. Of course, following the collapse, we then get to read about them in various rate fixing scandals like the LIBOR (London Inter Bank Lending Rate) being massaged and hedge fund managers and bankers receiving huge financial incentives and there is a huge public outcry because we perceive these events as threats. When this occurs, of course we illicit the threat response unconsciously and find ourselves feeling disgusted about the entire episode taking place.

The above is obviously a larger scale example of fairness being thwarted but what about the times you've been fleeced for an unfair parking ticket, an unwarranted speeding ticket or clamping fine on your car or an unusually high restaurant bill where you haven't actually drunk any alcohol but are then made to pay for the drinking excess of others in your party?

List or make a note of situations where fairness for you has been thwarted and when it happens again what will you do differently to cope and thrive better?

What happens inside your brain when basic SCARF needs aren't being met?

Naomi Eisenberger, a leading social neuroscientist from UCLA University of California, made some amazing discoveries from her work into personal rejection. Using FMRI technology she had her subjects play Cyberball, where individuals thought they were playing a ball tossing game on computers in their lab. The subjects were able to see a representation of themselves on the screen as an 'Avatar' playing the game with two other people. About halfway through the game, the two other Avatars stopped throwing the ball to the subject's Avatar and naturally the subject complained about being excluded from the game at this point.

In spite of later being told it was a programming function of the experiment for his Avatar not to be passed the ball and in fact none of his other college friends had actually been participants in the game, the subject continued to talk about feelings of anger, being snubbed or judged as if he'd been excluded from the game because there was something wrong with him or his personality.

All the while that this game was taking place, the students were each wearing an FMRI head set monitor and something rather interesting was occurring inside their brains. What Eisenberger and her colleague Matthew Lieberman saw was amazing because an area of the brain became very active during this high arousal period, this is known as the dorsal portion of the cingulate anterior cortex, an area linked to the suffering component of pain. What this reading was telling them was that being excluded from the game, left the subject feeling angered and disappointed by being ostracised by friends, was actually causing (in neurological terms) physical suffering in the subject! It was as if the subject's brain was interpreting this event much in the way as it would experience a physical beating from an attacker. The lower image of the subject shows the brain region lighting up when experiencing physical pain and the upper image shows the same part of the brain becoming active during the experimentation process.

SOCIAL PAIN

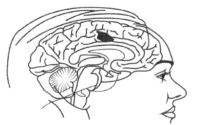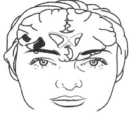

PHYSICAL PAIN

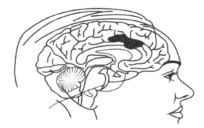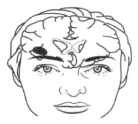

This significant discovery adds weight to the analogy of 'hurt feelings'. Furthermore from other research we know now that under hypnosis, the cingulate anterior cortex and emotional centres of the brain operate differently which allows patients to undergo surgical procedures without anaesthesia. Whilst the nerve receptors in the body, where the procedure is being carried out, continue to register the electronic signals to the brain (suggesting there is pain to be felt), it would seem that the emotional regions and anterior cingulate cortex processes the signals in a way that would allow patients to feel entirely comfortable during even the most invasive procedures whilst being hypnotised - this is also referred to as the 'placebo effect'.

You can watch a short video on youtube.com by typing in Perceptions of pain changing under hypnosis featuring Dr Michael Mosely, the scientific research correspondent for the BBC, receiving a series of painful electrical shocks and hear how his colleague in the film explains the effects of hypnosis on the brain, which allows him to reframe the experience of receiving the electrical shocks as rather more like warm sun tan cream being applied because his colleague is talking about Dr Mosely lying on a warm beach.

What the research by Eisenberger and Leiberman also shows is that the brain is a social device and our needs aren't just driven by basic needs like water, food, shelter, air and sun; our mind set can be altered and affected in many other situations too. Especially where our basic social needs are compromised - be that in a career role, in a family situation or with friends. It's vital that we have these needs met in order to avoid the melting down affect that threats can cause us to experience.

The Human Truths…

The constraints of the past impose themselves on your current thinking and affect the way you think about the future too.

Human beings are totally self-absorbed – they spend all their lives searching for evidence that validates their opinions of themselves…

That internal dialogue you have will always continue and if it's especially negative then just hang up…!

Session 2

This shit's just got to change!

Research from Benenden Health in 2013 revealed that the average Briton worries for up to 2 hours every day which is close to 5 years in a lifetime. Such a waste, I'm sure you'd agree.

The top stressors reported were mainly about modern living, including money, health, being overweight, job security, ageing and relationships. One in 10 reported that they feared opening bills, statements from the bank and similar letters and 45% of those questioned felt that stress had directly affected their health.

How can we begin to make this change exactly and how can I be so flippant in the face of these facts to say there's more right about you than there is wrong where you're breathing, have a pulse, appear conscious, etc?

It starts with knowledge about a part of the Ape brain that does all this crazy stuff and recognizing its motives and behaviours consciously so that when you find it kicking off you, or rather your frontal region, your modern brain, can spot this and begin focusing your attentions elsewhere.

What is the stress response?

The stress response could be a saviour; on the other hand it could be a killer too. It's all about the way in which you wish to view it. Naturally if you're subject to a 'HALTS' moment then you'll naturally be drawn to see it from a negative point of view on the other hand you're more likely to be able to respond more easily if you aren't 'hungry, angry, late tired or stressed out'.

When faced by a very real or perceived threat, humans have chemical reactions in the brain which are rapidly played out on in the body.

27

This stress response dates back many millions of years and it's there for a good reason, to protect us. It comes in several forms too: there's a fight/flight/freeze or fawn response which we'll examine as we go further into this section.

Let's go back in time, several million years and explore its origins. Of course, what threatened us then was very different to what threatens us now. I'll suggest back then by way of an arbitrary example, a threat of the sabre toothed tiger. We're part of a group of other hunter gatherers who have over several days existed on fruits and berries and vegetation and are on the hunt for meat because we're famished. We're in a forest, near a stream and looking for a wild boar. In nearby bushes, there's a sudden rustling followed by a wild roar and out leaps an equally hungry sabre toothed tiger also looking for meat…yours! I have already turned and run off down the track.

In that moment the sound and leaping animal causes you to freeze, which is one of the several responses you can have from a sudden shock. This point will often define how we respond the next time to the same stimuli too. So what happens next? Under circumstances where no perceived or actual threat occurs, the visually observed stimulus passes in your brain to the thalamus as you can see in the picture and should then pass to the occipital region at the back of the brain - for this to make sense visually, turn the image the right way up. Then the information will pass to the hippocampus for the purpose of indexing and memory - however, this is where there is little or no perceived threat. Which isn't what's happening to you; you're in great danger of being torn apart limb from limb because I have made my exit.

In the briefest moment where the threat is perceived like a sabre toothed tiger, the visual image in your brain is fast tracked to the Amygdala, a part of our Ape brain. This is the moment you freeze and have a reorientation response. Here, your amygdala almost instantly takes a metaphorical snap shot of the incident, recording all the detail of the situation ranging from loosely compiled information about the sights, sounds, smells, colours, any tastes and a whole load of information associated with this situation. It makes a comparison to what it already has by way of knowledge about these things and these can be very loose associations too. Your frontal brain region hasn't even decided what it's going to do about the tiger yet as the considered, rationalized response takes far too long. You've only got an instant to make your move at this point. The moment this recording process takes place then the amygdala will kick things into action. All of this happens in your brain, in the blink of an eye quite literally.

So what happens next is an amazingly complex orchestrated process.

Adrenaline (Norepinephrine) and cortisol are released into the blood supply. The adrenaline increases your heart rate and elevates blood pressure and boosts energy supplies whilst cortisol, the primary stress hormone, increases glucose energy in the bloodstream as well as enhancing the repair functions of the body. To not only escape but also to ensure we are less likely to suffer infection or bleed to death from our injuries.

So now the game is afoot because, of all the people in your hunting party, the sabre tooth has taken a liking to you and you're being chased by this sabre toothed tiger. Do you think your body needs to use non-essential functions? These are a waste of time; your entire body and brain are now focused on making good an escape as your body explodes into action to get away. Your respiration rate goes up wildly and background functions, things like digestion, reproduction and tissue repair and growth are suppressed. In the meantime, blood supply goes to your major organs in order to provide increased dynamic movement, your senses sharpen, thought speed increases dramatically so that the events appear to slow down in your mind, allowing you to see cues that help you decide what happens next, (we call this the car crash phenomena - if you're someone who's been involved in a car crash or some such similar incident you'll know what this is like). Additionally muscles in your body will become fuelled and are temporarily boosted. Your hands sweat in order to grip rocks or climb if necessary and hopefully all these things well co-ordinated, will help you and your friends in the group to make good an escape.

Your unconscious response on this particular occasion was to run, so you still haven't fed at this point. The next day, you go hunting again and armed with the amygdala's sensory early warning template, continually scanning for danger cues which are subliminally being cross checked and matched up, how do you think your body will be feeling? At best uneasy because the amygdala will be looking for clues about this environment that can alert you to dangers. It begins to do something quite amazing - 'pattern matching' - looking for places where there are forests, leaves, a running stream and the rustle in the bushes that are held on this template. The pattern match doesn't even need to be exact, it can be very loosely linked because after all this part of your brain is designed to warn you of threats and dangers.

So there you are in the jungle on day two and the bushes suddenly rustle again! What may happen? Probably you'll run away; however, on this occasion, as you head off down the trail, what appears from behind the bushes is the boar that you've hunted high and low for during the last few days. The threat perception of the sabre toothed tiger was so very high, your amygdala is now very, very sensitive to anything remotely linked to the stimulus recorded in the amygdala's memory template.

The point here is this!

Surely when the stimulus causing the fight or flight response has passed by, shouldn't the stress response itself diminish? You'd think so, wouldn't you, as this usually happens in other mammals like zebras and monkeys for example. Once they've been chased for 45 seconds they've either made good an escape and carry on with their existence to run another day or, they're torn apart limb from limb by the pursing lion pack.

In humans however, things couldn't be more different.

The stress response in humans, will it save us or kill us?

The stress response is clearly in place to help remove us from the immediate danger, this is a great strategy and is known as acute stress which in the short term does us no real harm. However, where stressful stimulus or the possibility of stressful stimulus continue to hamper our experiences, otherwise known as chronic stress, then we can find our stress responses continue to fire off more and more often and then our bodies' attempt to calm us down can in time become the very thing that starts to kill us!

The long term consequences of stress activation in the body have been well documented by many, many studies. Professor Robert Sapolsky of Stanford University, in his book, **'Why zebras don't get ulcers'**, describes this continuing activation process as *penny wise pound foolish* because what happens over the years is that the continual turning on and off of the stress response causes disruption of the body's processes. This is linked to things like chronic anxiety because you've got high levels of cortisol and adrenaline floating around the blood stream which take time to dissipate, allowing us to calm down.

Professor Sapolsky is world renowned for his studies of stress and links between primate social and living behaviours and the curious parallels they share with humans. He's travelled during the last 35 years plus, extensively to Kenya, East Africa and spends several weeks at a time watching, tracking and recording the pack behaviours of baboons which are often very similar to humans. According to Sapolsky's observations, the baboons spend 3 hours daily hunting food and if a higher status baboon, around 9 hours making other low ranking baboons unhappy! What is so interesting about his findings is that the baboons are not so much being stressed out by lions or similar animals ripping them limb from limb, they are being stressed by other baboons creating social and psychological tumult. This is the reason why they're so interesting as a comparative model to humans and I would go as far to say that in many ways, they are so much more like us in this area of behaviour than you or I might have previously imagined.

The stress response is our natural response mechanism to being pursued and equally we'd have used it to catch our own prey too. Zebras, like monkeys, respond with fight or flight reactions to stress when being chased but as soon as the chase is over and it's gotten away it is able to switch it off. Amazingly humans use the same stress response to worry about mortality, taxes, the mortgage, relationship issues, our weight and finances to name but a few!

Imagine if a zebra could speak English, what do you think it might tell you if it knew you were using the same endocrine reactions as it does to run from being eaten alive whilst you worry about what others think of you or your fear of public speaking?

It would tell you to 'Have a word with yourself, you aren't even doing your fight or flight responses for a real physiological reason either.' 'You and other people are doing it non-stop and some people are quite literally doing it several times a day which is completely crazy!'

We're many of us living in a civilised society so we ought not to then act out the fight or flight behaviours which means that we're forced to suck it up and, as a result of not turning off this response and not acting it out, like running wild in public places, it leaves us having to wallow in a chemical pool of hormonal secretions, that are largely left unspent. The stress response or our attempt to calm down after a stressful event can, after a while become more dangerous than the stressor itself!

As people succumb to this situation more and more, they can find themselves in a broader sense less and less able to deal with the more trivial situations which shouldn't be stressful but actually have caused their blood to boil! Make a quick note to yourself about this now.

5 trivial things that have gotten you a bit stressed out recently that really shouldn't have done:

Incident details	How do you feel about it all now and what would a Zebra tell you to do?

Positive Stressors

Equally we can find ourselves revelling too in the very same stress response when we're doing something incredibly crazy, novel and fun. Like doing a martial art, jumping from a plane or skiing and we call this stimulation, challenge or excitement.

The real goal in life shouldn't be to avoid stress, it's to be stressed by the right type of thing. We love it and in control terms, it should be a time-restricted stressor that we would happily pay money for because we give up some controls and we surrender ourselves willingly to potential dangers with a certainty of finally coming away from the situation unharmed and yet elated from the experience.

Think about 5 activities you have done or could do that you know will produce a positive stress response and make a brief note to yourself as to why you would see this as an exciting event as opposed to perceiving it as a threat situation.

Event	Write about why exactly you'd see this event as being exciting as opposed to stressful

Session 3

What's your personal relationship with stress?

Your ability to cope with the demands of life is the key to your perception of how stress impacts on you. Imagine if everything in your life is going well then the idea of starting work in a new job can be exciting however, in the event of you starting a new job when moving house, experiencing money problems or worse still, suffering from the death of a loved one, it can mean the same event can have extreme stress effects.

The Social Readjustment Rating Scale or what is now also known as the The Holmes and Rahe Stress Scale is a useful tool to measure your personal stress loading. I've found it useful for myself and clients too. It was first used in 1967 when psychiatrists Thomas Holmes and Richard Rahe studied 5000 medical patients to discover whether any of them had experienced one or more of 43 life events mentioned in their assessment during the previous two years. Each event is referred to a life change unit (LCU). Each LCU has a weighting for stress. The more LCU's you've experienced during the last 2 years, the more you add to your total stress loading value.

Take the Holmes and Rahe Stress Test using google and discover your personal stress loading, incidentally, mine was 203 at the time of writing this book which means I'll have to work on myself more too! Here's the internet link
http://www.mindtools.com/pages/article/newTCS_82.htm

Begin firstly by selecting the LCU's in your current life circumstances during the last two years and record the total value for each event then simply total up all values.

- If your score is 11-150 then you only have a low to moderate chance of becoming ill in the near future.

- If your score is 150-299 you could have a moderate to high chance of becoming ill in the near future.

- If you score 300-600 you could have a very high risk of becoming ill in the near future so first things first avoid immediately any life crises.

This may as a starter, require of you, choosing not to move house, perhaps learn conflict resolution skills to deal with people you are in dispute with for example. Avoid taking on new significant obligations like study programmes, major loans etc. Choose to take things easier and look after yourself, ensuring that you get sufficient sleep, whilst eating and alcohol consumption only be done in moderation. This is not medical advice as such but merely a guide. If you have additional questions about your health then please seek the advice of a suitably qualified practitioner.

It has been suggested quite reasonably that the Holmes and Rahe scale is not reliable for every culture as there are different values placed on these events. For example people living in Malaysia have differing attitudes to breaking the law and towards personal marital relationships than Americans, meaning that their experiences differed at the same points scores. It's worth remembering how your own values might impact on the ratings too.

It's also important to note that your scale score may be quite high but your own unique temperament will invariably play a part in how you see the situation. I was recently talking to a lady professional healthcare worker who's scoring was much higher than 400 because she was going through a major divorce and all the associated complications of this however, her outlook was based on the fact that this was a great release in her life, she was looking forward to a single life again and understood that this was a stressor limited to the specific circumstance and wasn't a permanent life experience. In other words think positive and don't dwell on your findings.

How long term chronic stress affect your health

To help make this less scary, let me start by suggesting that stress doesn't actually kill you! Chronic stress and the repeated activation of the fight or flight response has been shown however to affect the performance of your auto-immune system which in turn leaves you susceptible to the ravages of infections and diseases, some of which lead to death.

The myth of peptic ulcers and other stuff!

When I was a teenager, in the late 70's, my art teacher used to tell me that he had terrible peptic ulcers brought on by stress, rich spicy food and high levels of stomach acid. This was the common belief in medical practice. The cause of stomach ulcers were then linked by Australian researchers Barry Marshall and Robin Warren to a bacteria called helicobacter pylori which was present in most people's guts anyway. So why was it that some people got ulcers and others didn't? It was then discovered by researchers that it was those who were experiencing chronic stress and therefore reduced functioning of the auto immune system that were most likely to develop peptic ulcers. In other words the bacteria was allowed to run amok in the gut because the immune system under repeated chronic stress exposure was unable to counter this!

Increased blood pressure caused by the stress response damages artery walls over long periods and causes them to fur up - otherwise known as arterial sclerosis - which can of course lead to a heart attack if the plaque deposits lining the arteries break away, causing a blockage. This can lead to horrible consequences such as a stroke, brain aneurisms or a heart attack.

Sapolsky's work has shown us that rather like human systems, the baboons live in groups where there needs to be political savvy, where individual baboons know their own rank, they understand who they're answerable to and who answers to them. There's a hierarchy, just in the same way there are structures in human life too.

Amazingly from his research he discovered that baboons who had a high rank in the pack had less stress hormones in their blood than the lower ranking monkeys. Additionally they were in overall better health too, with lower blood pressure, better performing auto immune systems and reproductive capacities. Whilst the lower ranking monkeys had brain chemistry which was similar to humans (who were clinically depressed) and much higher levels of arteriosclerosis than those in dominant positions. Similar research conducted by Professor Carol Shively at Wake Forest University demonstrated similar results too.

And here comes the juicy stuff...

Stress's effects on the brain!

The effects of chronic stress also occur in many other areas. Let's look at the brain. We now refer in common language to the stress response causing 'emotional hijacking' - a term used by Daniel Goleman in his books on emotional intelligence. Quite literally under stress we become stupid - as I mentioned earlier, our modern brain shuts down and the limbic region takes over. Useful in high stake situations for short periods if necessary when under attack!

Chronic stress in the brain kills brain cells and shrinks the brain. The hippocampus is where our learning and memory areas exist and this is situated in the medial temporal lobe. Chronic stress, according to Dr Bruce McEwen at Rockefeller University, will affect your brain circuitry so we lose the capacity to remember stuff we need to know. In the short term this makes it difficult to remember stuff that is required for things like taking exams, especially if accompanied by a lack of sleep!

Chronic long term stress responses will also make people just plain miserable by reducing the production of a neurotransmitter called dopamine, which has been shown to bind to receptor cells in the brain linked to curiosity, pleasure and reward. So jokes that are hilarious to others don't make people who are stressed or even worse, depressed, laugh. People who are experiencing chronic stress or depressive episodes fail to notice the wonderfulness of other people who have a friendly demeanour or as I have seen myself, people in these situations don't even notice the brightness of the sunny day. You say to them what a lovely day it is today and they respond with 'Well, what's so lovely about it!' They don't notice how delicious food tastes or how green the grass looks because as you now know, they're paying attention to things that are more likely to be negative.

There is also evidence to suggest that stress has become a critical factor in the western world's global obesity problem and it's a growing problem that isn't just linked to diet or a sedentary lifestyle. But we'll come back to this a wee bit later. I want to talk about my favourite topic now!

Stress and sexual performance

We have two systems operating in our bodies, one is the sympathetic and the other is the parasympathetic nervous system. To demonstrate simply how the two work in balance, try this quick experiment.

Slowly breathe in through your nose, really take in a large nostril full of air and notice how this feels enlivening. That simply is your sympathetic system kicking in to spark you into life, your body shifts and for a moment you feel alert. Now breath out through your mouth and take a good 3-4 seconds extra making sure this time you exhale pretty much all the air out of your chest and even in your lower diaphragm and notice how your shoulders drop, your legs become relaxed and heavier too as your facial muscles relax also and you may even feel a little flushed. This is the relaxation response and naturally your body provides this through the parasympathetic system and for much of your day the two are competing in the body to balance you and the way you feel.

In order for a man to get an erection for example, there has to be a state of calm with the accompanying relaxation response operated by the parasympathetic system as well as the sexually arousing stimulus which are of course varied, based on the sexual interests of the individual.

41

So now we set the scene; your parasympathetic system is operating quite nicely thank you. There's a relaxed tone to the body. Things start rolling as whoever you're with, maybe you're on your own, or whatever you're doing together causes your breathing to increase, your heart to pump blood faster and in greater volumes. Your muscles tense from the pleasure, you begin sweating and all these things are beginning to turn on the sympathetic nervous system and reduce the operational performance of the parasympathetic system.

The sensations of this situation become more intense; you're increasingly turning on your sympathetic system and holding onto the last outpost of your parasympathetic system. All the while the sexy stuff is getting more enlivening until suddenly you switch off the parasympathetic system, causing a pleasure build up and orgasm, leaving you then to flood back into a relaxation response and post orgasmic glow. Note how all this started from the position of a relaxed state and then built up to a state of excitement.

What happens during stressful events is quite the opposite because you're in a state of high arousal from the start. It's difficult when nervous around a lover, to establish the parasympathetic state which leads to arousal but let's say from the start you are relaxed and then half way through the action, your mind begins to wander off the sex and onto something you've been worrying about? After all, you can worry about how well you'll perform or the worry of an unexpected tax bill can creep into your mind unexpectedly. This will then result in the sympathetic system firing too quickly ahead of schedule and results in sudden loss of functionality and disappointment.

The release of the stress hormone cortisol in the body plays a part, as it influences the release of hormones in the brain which reduce pituitary sensitivity and this goes on to affect the messenger signals travelling to the testicles. Beta-endorphin is another stress hormone; it's the brain's natural version of morphine and is closely related to pain regulation. This is also released, which affects both men and women but in men seems to be linked to reduced testosterone levels and a fall in sex drive.

Let's not forget then too that this unfortunate event where you fail to perform can be seen in the brain's circuitry as one of those rustle in the bushes, sabre toothed tiger events. This lets the amygdala fire off pattern matches that may link the prospect of future failures in erectile functioning, when the individual finds themselves back in the bedroom situation again especially when you're with the same partner!

Stress, obesity and its links to affluence …

Stressful events make around two thirds of us become hyperphagic which means we experience feelings of excessive hunger and increased appetite. Other people become hypophagic meaning they experience a significant loss of appetite, they can't touch a morsel and they appear to crash diet. (Laboratory rats seem to illicit similar responses to stress also!) When you congratulate people you know for dropping a few clothing sizes they tell you it's thanks to stress. I reckon you've probably met both types yourself.

So what's happening within the complex activity the body goes through during fight or flight, to make us sometimes prone to become fatter? Here's a quick easy style explanation of this process…

Corticotrophin-releasing hormone (CRH), is released by the Thalamus and it gets things really kicking off by stimulating another hormone (ACTH) adrenocorticotropin hormone. ACTH then stimulates the adrenal cortex in the adrenal gland, which causes a synthesis of gluccocorticoids including cortisol as well as several other hormones to be produced, in order to fuel the fight or flight actions. CRH is a very fast acting gluccocorticoid and plays an especially important role in increasing vigilance and arousal during stressful events (interestingly, it also suppresses appetite).

On the other hand, gluccocorticoids like cortisol appear to stimulate appetite. CRH diminishes quickly too which is fine because when the stressor stimulus has gone, it's gone. However the cortisol and other chemicals which stimulate appetite need some time, perhaps several hours to dissipate and will therefore, continue to affect us long after the stressor has exited. This is what you and I consider the recovery period and what do many people do after a particularly stressful event? Yes, of course, they turn to food, as a comfort following the stress because the body has supposedly got to refill again after all the energy has been burnt off from the fight or flight response. That would be all well and good though if you were being chased across an African savannah but most of us, including me, are much more likely to sit down and munch a packet of Scottish shortbread during the recovery period.

There is something else that needs to be there too which is key to our western capitalist lifestyles!!! Let me explore the idea that you work for yourself or maybe in an office and each and every day you are being exposed to situations that are stress inducing, for various reasons. What happens then to when you have the repeated switching on and off of the chemical process in and around fight or flight arousal, where CRH is introduced, disappears quickly after the stress inducing stimulus has gone, only to be replaced with Cortisol that may take several long hours to dissipate and spikes increased attention to needing to eat yet more food in order to recover?

Taking into account that some people have different stress triggers, body recovery capacities and differing coping mechanisms than others and what stresses one person a great deal, may only stress another person mildly, there's some fantastic work that has been done by Dr Elissa Eppel of the University of California, San Francisco and it shows that people who are hyperphagic as a result of stress specifically, tend to want to turn toward sweet, high fat content foods. Especially if their endocrine responses classified them as hyper-secretors of cortisol as opposed to those who had lower baseline responses under stress or are slower to recover from the stress response.

Now most people don't just eat for nutritional purposes, many of us like to eat as a strategy to cope with our emotions. Many of us are actively controlling our dietary intake however, what is apparent is that these very same people when faced with highly arousing, stress inducing situations lose control and become hyperphagic. We need to treat ourselves during the recovery stage of a stress inducing situation because when we're not overly stressed we can exercise control over our food intake but when we are stressed, we can't!

So her research shows that when not stressed, both emotional eaters who eat when stressed and non-emotional eaters who use food for nutritional purposes tend to eat the same at times of normality

46

however, when adversity falls hard upon them, then the emotional eaters tend to be a lot more at risk from over eating due to stress.

Anecdotally, I used to see chronic depressives in my private clinic who couldn't raise the energy to cook food for themselves and would often rely on takeaways and white bread, the food of convenience which required little or no effort and now seem to have poor nutritional value. The Whitehall survey also demonstrated that not only was obesity linked to stress and position in the hierarchy, it also appeared to show a correlation to how fat itself would be distributed in the body as you put on weight! It would seem from these findings that people lower down in the hierarchy were more prone to putting on the fat around the front of their bodies in their abdominal cavity. It is certainly apparent that this happens in monkeys who are dominated by others in the pack.

Researchers like Sapolsky, Shivley, Marmott and other scientists now seem to think that fat brought on by stress is actually more dangerous than fat accumulated by people who are moderately or less stressed but enjoy a high calorific intake. Fat carried in the abdominal cavity seems to act differently than other fat deposits in other parts of the body. They've seen that it behaves differently and produces different types of chemicals and hormonal secretions which have different effects on your health.

In researching these ideas, I was amazed to discover the number of overweight and obese adults in the developing world has almost quadrupled to around one billion since 1980. 64% of UK adults are classed as overweight or obese. Around the world the numbers of people who are obese or overweight have risen from 23% to an amazing 34% of the entire population between 1980 and 2008. A report from the Overseas Development Institute predicts a huge increase in diabetes, heart attacks and strokes which are not only caused by diet but stress factors too.

What's also coming to light is that the problem is growing so fast in emerging countries too and at a much faster rate than the first westernised countries; places like the Philippines, Mexico and Egypt where incomes are rising. It's apparent that across the world we're now seeing a growth of incomes and material affluence being linked to the rising incidences of obesity, diabetes and other lifestyle related issues. Wherever we are in the world and the wealthier we are feeling, the chances are that we're likely to be consuming more fatty foods and the sicker we're becoming too as a result of diet and stress related conditions occurring.

If you take America, around 15% of the population aged 65 were experiencing adult onset diabetes and this was certainly a major public health problem in 1990. A decade later this figure had risen by 33% and it was also observed that the occurrences were beginning to effect younger people too. Its type 2 diabetes that has become so prevalent that we have seen a 70% increase, for example in 30 year olds, during the last decade with adult onset type 2 diabetes. It would seem that adult onset diabetes has now become even more prevalent amongst young kids than the onset of juvenile type 1 diabetes.

This has led to people like Michelle Obama and Jamie Oliver suggesting that children alive today will die younger than their parents. Now I don't believe that this will be down to poor nutritional value diets alone. You look for example at the work of Sir Richard Peto, Professor of Medical Statistics from Oxford University, who balances this assertion by suggesting, 'That the probability of dying from the sorts of things caused by being overweight has gone down by a factor of four'. He also added, "If you go back 30 years then the chance we would die from a heart attack or stroke and diseases like that in middle age was 16% whereas it was 4% in 2010." It is certainly clear that poor diet, stress and other outside environmental factors like wealth or the perception of wealth, do impact greatly on our health and wellbeing and in the words of allostatic load specialist Joseph Meyer, 'Prosperity has become a cause of death.'

So the next question is why? I mean surely where there is an abundance of opportunity, prosperity and wealth we should thrive? Is that not a reasonable assumption? Shouldn't we be thinner, in better health? Apparently not, an Oxford University study says that people in wealthy countries with 'free market' economies are more likely to be obese.

The research of 11 affluent countries in 1994 through to 2004 compared obesity. The Oxford University researchers were keen to discover why those living in Britain and the US were heavier than people living in Norway and Sweden. To do this they looked also at research into animal behaviours which indicated that under stressful conditions, animals eat more, especially when faced with uncertainty. Remember certainty being one of the principle factors of SCARF which suggests that obesity is linked to social causes and not just poor diet in isolation!

So it's entirely possible that people when faced with uncertainty about life and money will be driven to overeating and this links obesity to monetary stresses in the UK and US. Professor Avner Offer, lead study author and Professor of Economic History at the University of Oxford in his study looked at 96 national surveys on obesity which were carried out over 10 years across a wide range of different countries and they examined 'Market liberal' nations including the UK, Canada, Australia and the US. These were compared to other countries that offered stronger social protection and higher levels of economic security through their state run/government run economic systems. These included Germany, France, Italy, Norway, Spain, Finland and Sweden.

The study concluded that countries with more market liberal economies have higher levels of obesity and obesity growth rates, around one third more than those with stronger social protection mechanisms in place. The US had the highest levels of obesity with a mean of around 30% obesity whereas Italy with the lowest obesity rates had almost half the US levels at 17%.

Professor Offer said, "Policies to reduce levels of obesity tend to focus on encouraging people to look after themselves but this study suggests that obesity has larger social causes.

"The onset and increase of large-scale obesity began during the 1980s and coincided with the rise of market-liberalism in the English-speaking countries. "It may be that the economic benefits of flexible and open markets come at a price to personal and public health which is rarely taken into account." So this may be down to market driven competition factors in certain societies and at the same time has undermined people's perception of autonomy and certainty.

People who have not and what they're stressed about...

In the United Kingdom there are, according to government stats in 2014, around 3.3 million households claiming various state benefits and the current expenditure on benefits and other associated support measures was £28 billion. During the last 6 years, the cost of living has risen by 28% and average earnings have lagged woefully behind at 9%. This has been as a direct consequence of worldwide economic factors since the crash in 2008. There are quite literally several million people living in a situation referred to as being below the bread line and they are often living on such meagre earnings that they now turn most weeks to secure funding from debt management companies and this has become a significantly troubling issue as to cause the current government significant worry.

Many single parent families for example are trying to get by and around 700,000 have to live on zero hour contracts, where there isn't any guarantee of work and will earn anywhere between £7,000 and £10,000 if they're lucky to bring up a family in an environment where child care costs have run out of control to such an extent that they have risen by a staggering 77% in the last decade. Which means many millions of families across the UK will also need to rely on state handouts too.

Consider with the changing climate that in the last few years the UK government has made significant attempts to cut and claw back state funded aid whilst overlooking the fact that they're not really actively pursuing the 5% super rich or the vast money making corporations as aggressively as they could or maybe ought to for that matter! Even as I write this, there's a massive row about HSBC banking group actively allowing rich elitist clients and corporations to squirrel away substantial funds into Swiss banking accounts. This has been a political policy for maybe 30 years which has naively allowed the rich to get richer and the poorer to get poorer in the belief that the wealth would begin to cascade down.

This of course hasn't happened which has led to a savage disparity between the rich and the poor that has been increasingly prevalent in recent years. Of course another factor that bears this out is when you go to places where economic uncertainty, low wages and socio-economic factors indicate people aren't doing so well and you start to see the increasing numbers of people who are experiencing obesity, diabetes, heart conditions and all the common stress related symptoms go through the roof - but more about that later.

People who have lots, and what they stress about...

So now we can begin to understand that the 'Have not's who could be considered to be poorer, under privileged people living in an affluent society, may be stressed out by money worries. That I understand. In fact most of us would relate to this but then what about the super wealthy? How does being really extraordinarily wealthy affect them? What do they worry about and are the things they worry about that much different?

The results of research in 2014 are illuminating about those in the UK who are multi-millionaires and those who come from an averagely prosperous background. Respondents told the Lincoln Financial Group they worried about having enough available money in retirement. The report showed that typically 53% of people they'd surveyed worried about having sufficient funds but 48% of millionaires admitted to having concerns about having enough money to live their entire lives in comfort. Clearly having more money and wealth doesn't mean you're not going to get distressed.

Additionally you can have a lot of money but you'll still be forced into worrying about your health too. It would be reasonable to assume that the super-rich would be able to afford the very best doctors and have access to the specialist hospitals which would result in better health -

however the rich do worry but not as much as their less affluent counterparts from lower socio-economic groups. 54% of the millionaires interviewed worry about their health compared to 57% of all those surveyed.

Loss of capital and being sued also caused the richest people to worry. What was especially interesting was seeing information from a survey by Prince and associates showing that fewer than 20% of people who held less than £1,000,000 had ever worried about being sued whereas 80% of people worth £20 million and more are constantly worrying about being the target of a law suit!

This is probably a reflection of my social status but they also worry amazingly about things like identity theft. Only half the middle class people interviewed actually expressed concerns whereas three quarters of the super-rich lose sleep over this. Thieves it would seem are more into scamming off those with good credit history than those who have already reached their credit limits. The monthly utilities bills aren't high on their agenda as such but they do worry about interest rates, the fluctuations in foreign currency values, stock and share prices and the value of property and what the Bank of England and the US Federal reserve are reporting. This will also occur despite the cleverest rich people hiring experts to manage their portfolios and day to day affairs.

Imagine also that these guys don't just have a job which like so many of us they worry about. They own and run major business empires! It's misery being told there's no longer a need for your skills but what about making a bad business choice leading to the loss of jobs for quite literally hundreds or in some cases even thousands of people. What will happen to them if their reputation is at stake too? Those in the public limelight like sports personalities, major business leaders, political figures and royalty can all be hauled over the coals these days and be subjected to a huge amount of ridicule from things like social media and it's amazing how quickly people can fall from grace. We're just witnessing the collapse of FIFA and possible improprieties that have occurred in international athletics as an example which shows how quickly the mighty can fall and the story is being played out across social media and traditional news sources hour by hour.

Of course like you and I, the rich also worry about their kids but their worries tend to be more about concerns that their fortunes will be spent on fast women, performance cars, expensive holidays, nights out and masses of other trivial luxuries.

In the US there are around 1.8 million households who have assets in excess of $3 million dollars and many of the families owning this will struggle as to how their money will get spent after the off-spring receive their inheritance. It's well understood that large inheritances can undermine ambition and determination in children of fortune. Why should the kids want to study hard or take on the hardship and graft of a job when they know that they will be accessing a trust fund or masses of inherited wealth? In reality the people who have striven to build these empires will understand that there is self-esteem and self confidence in succeeding in work but will their children see this too? Just gives them one more thing to worry about!

Amazingly too when it comes to rich people, like their counterparts, the 'have not's, they still feel that they need to keep up with the Joneses too. The branding of your university, the car you have, the size of your house, what clothes you wear, the restaurants you eat, in the job you do, who you are seen with in public places and how your marital life is working are all reportedly on the conscious horizons of super rich people! That said, the rich at the same time value simple experiences just as much as those who have not! So take a moment now and please go back for the briefest moment and re-read what I told you in page one and two at the start of this book.

One additional knock-on effect of having too much money for the super-rich is the effects that this wealth can have on their children's health. It's not enough to be a rich adult with money worries, it seems that this will inevitably affect the kids of the wealthiest too. There is significant evidence that shows children who come from wealthy families are increasingly more likely to develop mental health issues. Where parents are earning more than £100,000 a year, the kids are experiencing increased levels of neuroses which lead to criminal behaviour, drug taking and eating disorders. The drive for parents to be pushy puts them under relentless pressures and they are unable to cope with the demands of their overly aspirational parents. Professor Suniva Luthar of Arizona State University is a world expert in the field of child welfare where children have been nurtured by affluent parents. She suggests that the children of the rich are expected to excel and report a relentless sense of pressure due to the high octane pressure put on them by their parents.

Her findings are also supported by Tanya Byron who is an eminent British psychologist who teaches young people to cope in her London clinics. A number of the students she sees going to high achieving independent schools have developed school phobias because they are afraid of failure and suffer from a range of additional conditions such as anorexia, depression and self-harming and it would appear that these incidences are more prevalent than at any other time in her long career and whilst she stresses that young people from poorer families are at greatest risk, it is apparent that young children belonging to rich parents are increasingly at risk too. According to her latest research, studies show that on average, serious levels of depression and anxiety symptoms occur twice as often amongst the children of wealthier parents compared to national rates. Of course the expectations of the parents are one side of the equation for this, there are the additional factors of expectation transmitted by the community, teachers, schools coaches and peers according to Professor Byron.

It's really clear that super-rich people do enjoy amazing lives and material prosperity but their woes, although not the same as the 'have not's, don't seem to make their experience of life necessarily much easier either. So what we have going on is a question of perception as much as anything. You may be a millionaire living in a neighbourhood of other millionaires but if their houses are £5 million pounds and yours is only worth a meagre £2 million, it's likely that this will be a stressor because it's not just being rich it's about also if you're doing as well as others living around you and who you compare yourself with that will promote a stress response. Conversely those living in a neighbourhood where you have low socio-economic status, then these people will not only be poorer in monetary terms, they will also feel poorer and this is just as stress-inducing as the dilemma faced by their wealthier neighbours. Which reminds me of a saying I used to hear, 'You can spend your time going around in misery but having a lot of money makes the misery just a little more bearable.' Or does it?

Consumerism, acquisition anxiety and possession obsession

We've fallen for this one hook, line and sinker too, as we've become increasingly primed by conditioning to link our status to the goods we have and the stuff we own. The advertising industry here in the UK, to give you a sense of scale, is valued at around £14bn annually and people around the world are hypnotised into buying trances, orchestrated by the clever marketing techniques of advertisers who now utilise even cleverer 'priming techniques' to cause us to buy stuff we don't even need, often unconscious of what programming takes place around us.

To illustrate this, try watching another Michael Moseley film clip which features the priming phenomena. If you look it up on YouTube, simply type in: 'The science of young ones-priming.' It'll make you wonder, I mean really wonder how much of this is taking place, especially when you consider that around 80% of what we absorb isn't even at the conscious level according to some of the very latest insights from thought leaders in this field.

Since the 1950's, our desire to purchase luxury goods has been unprecedented and yet our overall happiness levels are at such an all-time low. Scientific studies show that what we have and how much we own has little impact on our reported happiness levels. Professor Paul Dolan in his book, 'Happiness by Design,' illustrates this and additional research undertaken by Knox College in the United States has shown that our happiness, wellbeing and relationships have been negatively affected by possession obsession.

This trance state is induced by an initial belief that our lives will be so much better if we buy or owned product A, B or C and this massive marketing system is not only in overdrive it's going massive. The exponential jump in pace is being driven by the speed of social media. Facebook, Google, Twitter and all these systems now use wide ranging digital algorithms to track your mobile searching choices on the internet, just like an Orwellian 'Big Brother' and you can find something you searched an hour ago suddenly pops up and you then have micro-targeted influences pricking your attention, sitting there just on the peripheries of your awareness, awaiting some banal stimulus that prompts the purchasing decision at a later point.

This has become so powerful that we're not just spotting something we like that another person walking past us in the high street is wearing, or a friend has, we're now beginning to track, stalk and 'Like' or 'Follow' particular brands. We observe the behaviour of our friends using social media and when they post up an image of themselves in their new car, their holiday destination or eating at their favourite restaurant, we utilise their social proof to inform our behaviour and then this develops into 'Instagram envy' according to Professor Dolan. Also think about what I said earlier about dopamine being a chemical that is produced in states of arousal around sex, drug taking, curiosity, satisfaction, pleasure and interest for most of us, the act of shopping is similarly alike for many people. Apparently dopamine is also at its highest when you get your credit card out to make the acquisition - after all doesn't shopping get you feeling so much better about yourself?

Research done at Emory University by neuroscientist Gregory Burns and other leading researchers, has shown dopamine to be at its highest in the anticipation of the purchase, which reveals the idea behind why people are spending hours window shopping or nowadays surfing the internet for their next purchase, because there's an increasing excitement about the experience of acquiring the goods, there's novelty and newness switching from one iPhone to the next version out there and you talk to your friends about it, maybe they've even got one too! Of course on the downside something interesting happens the moment they have the goods in their clutches. Think about the neural high for a moment and people can find themselves mistakenly and emotionally, making sometimes terrible purchase decisions too. Which explains why people buy the shoes and white goods that they then never ever wear or use again. The average UK household has around £3500 worth of unused clutter and in 2014 Britons spent around £1.2bn on things they've never used.

Dr Berns said that, 'You see the shoes, you get this burst of dopamine.' He suggests that this is the motivation to 'seal the deal' and buy them. It's like a fuel injector for action but once they're bought it's almost a 'let down.' This let down is best known as 'buyers' remorse' where you then switch your attention away from the reward and toward the threat as the realisation occurs that you have spent more than you planned and there's still too much month left at the end of the money.

His research has also been conducted on rats who were exposed to new environments and compartments in their cages. This raised their excitement levels and their dopamine too which may explain why the act of shopping in a brand new shopping centre, can play havoc with your wallet and your intentions because time and again, we so easily fall foul of the all natural chemical high! That is unless, the mall is packed out with people, there are delays waiting in the queue plus perceived poor service from overwhelmed sales assistants and now an increased awareness of buyer remorse. This reminds me of some of the seasonal sales come to mind and just so long as the sale price saving is big enough we'll do our best to put up with the getting up at 6.00am the long queue, the rush for the best bargains and the pushing and shoving etc.

Trouble is that it's not so long ago that we had the 2008 credit crisis which left entire swathes of western society reeling. In the UK for example, the cost of living has risen 4 times faster than average incomes and research last year showed we were as much as £2234 worse off than three years ago. So in addition to the shopping dependency and its roller coaster effects, many people are on a course of behaviour that they can ill afford and then the final twist in this tale comes when people begin 'hoard games'.

All the stuff you have around you, in your home that you spent your hard earned money on can come back to haunt you. Women's stress levels according to the University of California, Los Angeles, hits an all-time high when confronted by the unused clothing clutter, especially when they finally decide to try and sort it all out and they have to mentally rake themselves over the coals about the stuff they bought and didn't wear which reminds them of their loss of mind and money, creating regret and additional anxieties. Although I haven't myself seen research on this, I think the same can be said for the men too; they'll either lament poor purchasing decisions they've made and if not they'll lament the decisions made by their partners.

So knowing that the shopping experience chemically alters your brain and can get you into all sorts of untold stress situations, I'd like to offer some thoughts about how you could avoid succumbing to this.

Firstly you might choose to define and write down a statement which best describes your identity. Then write down why you want the item and how this aligns to your identity statement. So if you've gone with a brand statement about your identity which might be, 'I am independent, creative and smart and I know how to get things done,' you're less likely to buy something that doesn't align itself to who you really are and it's much less likely you'll succumb to impulsive designer dead weight labels that you're buying just because your friend has it or one like it!

Defining who you are makes you less likely to follow the social proof of others and engage in flock-like buying behaviours. Buy from a pre-planned shopping list so you can avoid the impulse, dopamine-induced buying act. Only use cash and not a debit or credit card so it's real money you're handing over, not the plastic. Window shop after the store has closed and you've left your wallet and purse at home - you'll get the initial pleasure without the risk of spending and you can take the week to decide if this purchase will really make you happy. Consider, do I really need it? What are the implications of me not buying it and if the pros still stack up against the cons a week later, then it's a better choice you're making than the impulsive dopamine behaviour.

Researchers have found that around 68% of people who've been hoodwinked by the impulsive purchase would have opted for the wait and see if they'd known about it. If you do decide to splash out, maybe consider then changing your purchase choice, rather than a dress, new shoes, a bigger car etc, maybe consider booking a short holiday which is experientially driven and could provide you with much greater levels of joy and happiness as opposed to the outfit you picked up in the local shopping centre which you only managed to wear just the once.

Job and workplace stressors

Whatever work you do, there will at some point be some stress involved, which for the most part is positive and causes you to get things done. In the UK around 400,000 people experience stress-related illness linked to workplace stress. Samaritans UK, the charity that provides help and advice to people from all walks of life, found that 'people's jobs are the single biggest cause of stress' with around 36% of Britons feeling it was their biggest source of stress. People can face up to many challenges in life, however as the 40 year old Whitehall Civil Servants' survey reveals, their ability to cope changes quickly. The circumstances that will initiate this include when you feel you're being overworked, underpaid, bullied, have little opportunity for autonomy, dissatisfaction, newly introduced working practices that aren't sufficiently thought through, constant change and a fast working pace, leave most people floundering. Then you throw in job security, an economy that's under a lot of pressure and companies cutting back with redundancy. This only serves to add uncertainty and as the evidence shows, increases fear and increasing stress levels. The way you go about handling work place stressors that could become or are a problem, involve you choosing to pay attention more to what you can control, as opposed to what you can't.

Feeling overwhelmed by your occupation can erode your confidence, reduce personal productivity as well as your effectiveness and make the work you do seem less rewarding. So it's most important that you recognize the signs of excessive workplace stress to start with. These include; apathy and loss of interest in your work, problems sleeping, excessive fatigue during the day, struggling to concentrate, muscular tension, stomach and bowel problems, excessive alcohol consumption, loss of sex drive, feeling anxious, easily irritated or extended periods of moodiness and general depressive feelings.

Stressed by your status, job role and position in the organisational hierarchy?

It's amazing to think that the job you have in itself can be a source of stress but even more interesting than that is the fact that the position you hold within a business organisation can also be a significant contributing factor to how much stress you are likely to be experiencing.

The Whitehall experiment on stress levels of UK civil servants which even today, is now in its second stage, have been undertaken by Sir Michael Marmott and colleagues of University College London. For over 40 years since 1967, across 28,000 or more staff, they have revealed that those in this government agency who lived the life of a subordinate are often more prone to the pressures of excessive workloads, feeling overworked, undervalued and bored and the challenges this posed. Whilst those in higher ranking positions, managing sometimes up to 160 people in their department, described their jobs as enjoyable, challenging, exciting and dynamic.

The studies showed that the lower you are in the Whitehall hierarchy, the higher the risk of mortality, heart disease and other associated diseases including obesity, arteriosclerosis, diabetes, etc. The results were so stratified that those who were in the second to highest places had worse health than those at the top and those third down were in worse health than those in second position, right the way down to the people nearest the bottom.

This research shows that your working position or perception of this was intimately related to your overall health and wellbeing. Amazing to think that these people have the same levels of medical care and similar work roles - I mean it's not like the lower ranking workers are all doing hard manual labour like living back in the industrial revolution! They're not pushing coal trucks or being subject to severe beatings by way of workhouse reprimands but the lower down the hierarchy they are, the worse their health prospects become.

But let's just think about your own working role for a moment. When you examine the SCARF concept, what is happening? For example let's say you may work in a service based industry, most of us in some way already do, we all provide some kind of service to others in our work. What are your hours like, do people you work with treat you kindly, what effects do budgets and staff shortages have on you? Do you find yourself doing paperwork that not only is mundane but seems totally pointless too? How much job security do you have? Are there fat cat bosses working in your organisation who get more than they appear to be worth? Do you get paid a fair wage? Are you forced to work with people who you think are fools and you could do a much better job of it? All these things can affect you and your health especially the lower ranking in an organisation you feel or perceive yourself to be and the less control you appear to have.

That said, you might be a low ranking administrative assistant but in the evenings you might be captain of the company's quiz team or you organise the fun nights out or are the 'go to' person when others in your firm are in dispute and you harmonise. What I'm getting at here is again about perception because if your job brings fulfilment and status then it has meaning. To test that, I recently took a six week job working with a friend at a coffee van which was really badly paid, early hours and could have been a nightmare. What however gave the work meaning was the opportunity to meet some of the nicest people you could hope to meet and once they had their cup of 'Old Joe,' their trip into the city (even despite the lack of seating, early hour and onslaught of what was often seen as a 'boring job'), they'd really perk up and for me it was heaven on earth.

Perhaps if you find yourself like many, many other people in this situation, why not look at what meaning does your current role bring to you or perhaps other people? To amplify this I can tell you that I had major concerns about writing this book myself and it was the thought that if I didn't write the book, how many people would suffer from my indolence if they didn't get one or maybe two tips to help them improve their lives too? Before reading on can I ask you sincerely to jot down a few notes to yourself on this - it'll make you feel a hell of a lot better!

Coping with stress through exercise

So in the first instance, taking regular exercise is a great starting point despite it being the last thing you often actually want to start doing. This will boil down to anything that gets your heart rate pounding and you sweating and just about still able to talk afterwards. It's useful to take this type of thing one step at a time. Choose an activity you enjoy doing and you'll soon notice that you are feeling more energetic, in a better mood and more optimistic. I used to recommend my depressed clients did 20 minutes of fast vacuum cleaning around the house and then try to think depressed. It became difficult for them to focus on their depression because one of the things that happens is when you exercise you magically release endorphins which improve mood. Ironic really, prescribing a depressed patient more of the same thinking and catastrophizing don't you think? It's referred to as 'symptom utilisation' and worked surprisingly well too because endorphin production isn't usually associated with the depressed mind; you're more likely to find the person who is depressed has high levels of glucocorticoids floating around so focusing on negatives becomes difficult. At a psychological level, this reminds people who are depressed that their depressive episodes aren't a matter of permanence, they come and go and they're often not as long lasting as they may lead themselves to believe.

Why stick with exercise - it's so painful isn't it?

Commentators suggest that around 30 minutes of moderate exercise on a daily basis is a great base to work from. Trouble is though that it bloody hurts, especially if you're not someone who does or has done it on a regular basis. Let's take something straightforward like a jog or perhaps if you just don't ever do exercise, power walking! You start running and your body starts to say, 'What the hell are you doing??? You haven't run in years. What are you trying to do…Kill me?' So you get muscle ache, cramp, shortness of breath, aching arms, sore knees and just about anything else the body can come up with to stop you doing the exercise. Then your pseudo rationalisation of this starts kicking in. Your brain starts with things like, 'exercise is boring, I don't have time in my life to fit it in, it's too wet, and it's too warm'; one client told me that 'it was to medium!' Or my favourite which is, 'I work a full day and by the time I get back from a hard day on my feet, the last thing I want to do is more exercise'.

Let me let you in on something then. Undertaking aerobic exercise is after all a stressor on the body but it's one you're in control of and have decided to enter into voluntarily or maybe begrudgingly. One of the interesting things that short term stress can do is produce chemical opiates in the brain which after a short time begin to dull the pain of exercise. Stress induced analgesia is more common than you might imagine too. Let's say you're a serving soldier who's in the midst of battle and you're injured in the leg which almost certainly will be painful but not life threatening. Imagine the difference in this situation when the medic tells you that it's your lucky day because the injury sustained will become your ticket home to make a full recovery with lots of medical assistance and nice, clean sheets and plenty of care and attention from the medical staff.

You may not be a soldier so maybe a more common example is having athletic sex with a partner. There you are performing mind numbing gymnastics during this and it's resulting in your knees being grazed red raw on the poor quality carpet or on the table you've found to do the deed upon and of course during the event you really don't notice the pain as it's a pleasurable experience and your mind is being over-run by many wonderful endorphin infusions. What about running and other such aerobic exercises though, the first twenty minutes is usually where it feels like an act of pious self-flagellation for all your sins and then you actually begin to start feeling euphoric as the analgesic infusions of endorphins and other naturally occurring opioids kick in, hence what is described as the 'runners high'.

The whole episode then can take on a new meaning because you find yourself thinking, even contemplating making this a regular thing and you make a promise to yourself to lose weight and get fitter and live a happier, more productive life. Except for the fact that you wake up the next day feeling like you have been carrying around huge sacks of coal and your body will ache as your muscles cry out during their recovery. Don't worry too much because the body starts after say six weeks to get the hang of this process and beings to recover from the exercise more quickly. Additionally, people who regularly exercise report having greater focus, clarity of thinking, feel that they can use exercise to expend the build-up of glucocorticoids following a stressful day.

Remember all the stuff created by stress and floating around? This need to be flushed out and exercise is a great way to get this to happen. Of course if that's not in itself a great convincer, then consider that most people who exercise regularly feel they are less likely to be overwhelmed by events because their overall mood and perception of life is better and often report having more energy to get stuff done too as well as sleep better.

If however the idea of exercising say 5 times a week for 30 minutes seems just way too much all at once, you could start out with two fifteen minute sessions at different parts of the day. Maybe build up in the first instance with short walks if you've not done any rigorous training in a while. Exercise tends to become a habit rather than a chore if done regularly after about 30 days and you can begin upping your effort and activity levels as you see fit. Try doing different programs of exercise that will get you out of breath but still just able to talk. Focus on something too that you know you'll really enjoy. I enjoy running, dancing, karate and most days lift resistance hand weights for several minutes to provide a wide and varied range of physical activities. This may be something you'll try too but like I said, any exercise is always going to help more than none at all when it comes to managing your ability to cope with the stressors in your own life. I recently also watched a movie clip describing how to make exercise, in the first few weeks and increasingly regular habit and it's all about starting really small and building from there, associated to another behaviour you do a few times in the day. Imagine one simple example is when you go to the toilet, how about starting with 1-2 press ups immediately after. Suppose you go the toilet in your home 5 times per day imagine in one day you may have done 10 press ups and the rest is potentially plain sailing from there.

{Footnote} Some of the most recent research on exercise about what type of exercise burns fat fastest was undertaken by Benito Pedro et al 'Change in weight and body composition in obese subjects' Journal of applied Physiology 2015. Were they took 96 obese people and completed a 22 week supervised course of various kinds of exercise, in conjunction with a calorie restricted diet. The group were divided into 4 teams, some who did weight training, cardio such as jogging and sprints with other types of interval training and some who did weight training and cardio together as well as one further group who did light movement throughout the day like going upstairs at their workplace as a substitute to using the elevator and brisk walking. The diet itself was the same for all groups too. All subjects lost 9-10 kg of body fat and the resulting conclusions revealed that most of the factors were down to nutrition. Calories in and calories out is one of the biggest factors who need to lose a large amount of body fat and not whether you do cardio, weights or gentle movement like I mentioned above. Of course if you are already leaner before beginning the exercise the result would vary but gentle movement is just as effective in fat loss for people who are overly obese as doing crazy intense cardio circuits and or weight training sessions.

Stress and how this affects ageing

Whilst reading this book will make you a whole lot smarter about stress management, we're not getting any younger and the modern lives and choices about what we do and what we eat play a significant part in our ageing process. We now understand that stress affects everyone at genetic level, especially in the ageing process. If you take a DNA chromosome strand and look at it at a molecular level, you can observe that each DNA strand has what could be described as a sheath or telomere on the ends.

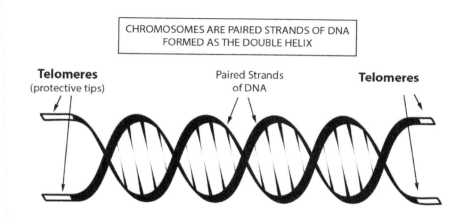

CHROMOSOMES ARE PAIRED STRANDS OF DNA
FORMED AS THE DOUBLE HELIX

Telomeres
(protective tips)

Paired Strands
of DNA

Telomeres

As we age, our telomeres shorten and stress hormones accelerate the rate of shrinkage. Humans have 46 chromosomes which are capped off by telomeres. Scientific research by Doctor Elizabeth Blackburn and Psychologist Elisa Epple into mothers of children with physical and mental handicaps, where of course there's an awful lot of stress, shows that the shrinkage rate of telomeres was directly linked to the amount of stress experienced, the time stress has been experienced and how frequently they experienced stress. The shrinkage as well as being linked to ageing was also linked to an increased risk of cancer cells developing too.

Being a mother or a father for that matter, with young children is often highly stressful; they have many competing priorities and perhaps struggle to deal with their own needs too. Then add into this the fact that the child is handicapped and chronically ill, showed that not only did the telomeres shorten quicker, the mothers died sooner too. Especially those who actually felt they were under enormous pressure to deal with the children. Assessments made by Blackburn and Epple suggest that for every year of looking after the handicapped chronically ill child, you were getting anything up to 6 years worth of ageing in the mothers. Scientific research could see that this accelerated ageing syndrome was caused by stress at a cellular level.

Dr Blackburn went on to discover an enzyme called Telomerase which was shown to repair the damaged telomeres and this healing effect appeared to come about when the mothers spent time sharing their concerns with each other and talked with each other about their issues, had a meeting of minds, even shared some forms of black humour about the situation. Now this raises a question, what are the ingredients in reducing stress and promoting wellbeing and longevity that are so important? It would seem to be compassion and caring for others actually does have after all a greater health benefit that we might imagine at a cellular level. Interestingly you can see why people might say, 'a problem shared is problem halved'.

So the next question is, exactly how does stress, poor diet and ageing affect the appearance of your face for example in terms of the ageing process. I found this fantastic article in The Mail Newspaper (type in to Google "Mail online what's stress doing to your face?") which explores what long term stress and a poor diet over 10 years does. Additionally you can also review the work of Auriole Prince who is an ex-FBI forensic artist. She has experience of working with investigators on ageing images of missing persons in order to be able to show what they may look like today.

She has developed several clever smart phone apps which will also show what your face looks like in the next 10 years, if you are a smoker or drink alcohol to excess regularly. Visit her website for more information www.changemyface.com it's really brilliant and a little weird, to see one self-ageing in this way!

What stresses the mother stresses the child

Stress on a long term basis is so toxic and far reaching in its ability to affect people; it can even impact the health, wellbeing and even the life expectancy of unborn children too... Tessa Roseboom is a Dutch researcher who studied in great detail an event in 1944 which was referred to as 'the Dutch Hunger winter'. Primarily this is where German Occupation forces during the winter, starved the Dutch population who went on strike over producing munitions and working services for the occupying forces. Being starved is a major source of stress and Roseboom wanted to see if the unborn foetus was affected by this stressor.

Roseboom found 2400 women who had been pregnant during this period. They were able to analyse the data and looked at babies born during and shortly after the famine. She wanted to discover if there were likely to be any longer term effects.

Her conclusions were surprising and shocking as many of the children born during the famine are now in their sixties and she found that many have increased risk of cardiovascular diseases, increased cholesterol levels, are more responsive to stress and had worse general health than those born before the famine or indeed conceived after it. Stress hormones in the mother's blood affected the nervous system and the brain chemistry and development of the unborn children as they and their mothers struggled with starvation. Over sixty years later they appear to still be fighting the battle.

It's apparent that the unborn foetus influenced by the stress hormones inside the starving mother, learned some really harsh lifelong lessons about famine. They developed 'thrifty metabolisms' which have resulted in them forever more being able to consume food and as a result of this imprinting experience, their bodies seemed, from very early childhood, to have made every attempt to hold on to as much of the food they consume, just in case there's another famine. So that in later life they have gone on to develop increased risk of obesity, adult onset diabetes, hypertension and cardiovascular diseases, plus an increased risk to all sorts of challenging mental issues that may or may not come to pass.

That's not the only thing to consider, because you take the prenatal child, a girl who has 'thrifty metabolism', grows up and becomes pregnant too. Her body running this strategy will possibly then go on to expose the unborn baby to mild malnutrition and bang - you have a chain reaction into the next generation. This of course isn't simply explained by it being a genetic thing; this is a reaction that is caused environmentally due to the exposure of the foetus to the mother's own blood supply which was filled with stress hormones that then affected the unborn baby.

It's certainly clear that prenatal stress experienced by the mother will directly influence the unborn foetus as it learns about the outside world through the endocrine system of the mother. When you have a mother who's stressed during labour, the baby is more likely to learn to become more susceptible to stressors following birth and into adulthood due to them learning life lessons in the womb and in their formative years. This exposure to pre-natal stressors can go to affect their base line resting glucocorticoids production, it also affect the rate at which they in later life can recover from stress inducing events and can put them at greater risk of longer term health complications including obesity, hypertension, cardiovascular disease, insulin resistant diabetes, reproductive impairment, heightened anxieties and impaired brain development relevant to learning and memory. In some extreme cases, even the onset of stress dwarfism in older kids around the ages of 5-6 years as well as bone disintegration and osteoporosis in adults too.

Post-natal stress responses in children

King Frederick II of Sicily who was knocking about in the early 1200's was renowned for his interest in science. He'd even had a prisoner locked into a casket and then observed to see if his soul would make an attempt to escape upon the moment of his death. Perhaps his most famous experiment was when he took a bunch of young babies and had each one reared in a room of their own. The kids would receive fresh food, bed linens, bathing and suckling, however the maids would not speak to the children. It was some far-fetched notion the king had that the kids would grow to speak the natural earth language which was Hebrew. Far from it, they all died! According to his friendly local friar and scribe, Salimbene di Adam, 'He laboured in vain, for the children could not live without clapping of the hands, and gestures, and gladness of countenance, and blandishments." This tells us that new-born kids don't just need a full belly of food, they need kindness, words of attention, a smile and to be picked up for a cuddle and a look into the eyes of the loving caring adult because from the very first moments in life they're learning stuff.

Dr Gabor Mate MD in his lectures, talks about the first few days of his young infant life in Hungary when at the time, the Germans were committing mass genocide on the Jewish population during the Second World War. The gist of the story goes that his mother speaks to the local doctor and tells the doctor that Gabor, her new-born baby boy has been fretting all night long. The doctor tells her that all the Jewish babies are fretting. Of course Gabor and all the other Jewish babies have no idea what's going on and aren't aware of the Germans, they're not aware of their atrocities either for that matter but they were all busy picking up on their parents' stress responses and learning from these too.

Early childhood stress and trauma can in some cases produce the primary enablers that lead to the onset of many of the conditions, which I've already talked about occurring later in life.

There's more though, there's the example of the infamous Romanian orphanages too. Under President Ceausescu it was strictly forbidden for women to have an abortion of an unwanted baby - this wasn't helped either because contraception was also banned. Birth rates increased as you'd expect but the knock on effect was that many young children were abandoned and often institutionalised into orphanages alongside the disabled and mentally ill too. Neglect, physical and sexual abuse plus the use of drugs to control the children's behaviours was common place, there were little or no washing facilities and medicines were in very short supply too. It wasn't until 1989 when the world became acutely aware of the problems and the outside world was entirely shocked to such an extent that numerous charities engaged in fundraising to help their plight.

Indeed part of Romania's conditions to entering the European Union was that they had to de-institutionalise them. Even though by 2011 there were still reports of poor conditions and large numbers of children still remaining institutionalised and traumatised in the most awful conditions. It is hoped that with the Romanian Child Protection systems and considerable charitable support these homes will be out of existence by 2020. The reason for mentioning this was that if you took a child who'd been adopted from one of these homes more than a year before, they'd still be showing very high levels of glucocorticoids production even in resting and recovery states despite receiving much attention from their newly founded and often deeply loving parental caregivers.

What influences whether or not you learned to be good at handling stress?

Scientists studying rats know that newly born rats licked by their mother, appear to develop much better psychologically than young rats that receive little or no attention at the point of birth. They are still fed the same foods and given sufficient watering, only to often be more susceptible to anxiety and experience greater levels of cortisol in their blood and all the other horrible stuff I have mentioned previously. But what of young children, what is it that happens for them that gives them a good base start for living potentially positive and productive lives?

Rhesus monkeys were studied by psychologist Harry Harlow of the University of Wisconsin; he was keen to discover the reason why exactly the infant monkeys became closely bonded to their mothers. The initial association was because she provided food. His research however, told us different because Harlow had actually built two pseudo mothers, both constructed of wood and a wire mesh designed to resemble a torso. In one there had been inserted a bottle of milk, this surrogate was providing nutrition. The second surrogate had a similar head and torso but instead of the milk bottle, the torso was wrapped in a warm terry cloth too.

It was thought that the baby monkeys would go for the milk but this proved not to be the case as the baby monkeys tended to choose the terry cloth mother instead, for as many as 17 hours per day with only 1 hour spent drinking from the bottle bearing mother. It would seem that kids don't love their mothers just for the milk and nutrition, it would seem that they love them because the mother or care giver appears to love them back, or at least in the very early period of their lives, providing immediate emotional support and interaction. "Man cannot live by milk alone. Love is an emotion that does not need to be bottle- or spoon-fed," wrote Harlow. You can view more about his amazing work on YouTube by typing in: Harlow's Monkey Studies or simply clicking the link above.

Research done by Tiffany Field of the University Of Miami School Of Medicine, along with Schanberg Kuhn who visited neonates and premature babies who were kept incubated in these wards at the time of the experiments and there was only minimal physical contact with the baby. Field and Kuhn began for as little as 15 minutes, 3 times daily stroking the bodies of the premature babies and moving their limbs. The resulting effects were almost miraculous because the babies began growing and developing 50% faster than babies who remained fed, nourished and yet untouched. They were observably more active and alert and went on to be released from hospital several days sooner than the neonates that remained untouched and months afterwards were doing better behaviourally.

So not only is food and warmth, accompanied by bathing, a part of child rearing, it's also down to the exposure that children have to being touched, picked up and held just as much as the other factors above. It's also about time being taken to nurture a child, have them spoken to softly, played with and given undivided and unstressed attentions of a care-giving or loving adult or parent. What is it about all this stuff that's so important exactly?

Think about the last time you picked up a new-born baby. If you haven't then try it, the effect is totally weird. You gaze down into its bright eyes and it looks back at you in wonderment with a fixed stare and then smiles…

In that instant, you're being hit by a quick fix of brain altering happy chemicals including endorphins, oxytocin dopamine and serotonin. The best bit is that these are all the natural feel-good chemicals which create not just a wonderful shared moment or a sense of bonding, healing and relatedness; they also carve out a new neural connectivity which affects the modelling of the brain itself. I like to think inner healing comes too when you're truly connected with another person. The same thing happens to the baby and you are now seeing a mutually beneficial effect on each other's brain chemistry. The baby gurgles and smiles more, your neural circuits are firing nicely in the limbic brain as you have several emotional reactions and blip - here comes another flush of dopamine too which raises your curiosity in the little infant even more. You start to talk in a funny voice to it and parts of its brain fires off things like dopamine and oxytocin which are again creating millions of little funny things called receptors for dopamine, oxytocin and other opiates. The receptors will also act as communication enablers between the 86 million neurons we're believed to have and as if by magic, a newly born baby will then begin playing a game of mimicry too, developed by nature's strategies, which mean it will copy your facial expressions, enabling you to respond and inevitably feel closer still as you can see here in the image:

We're mammals who get most of our brain's behavioural programming from the environment. Through our evolution from chimps, we've developed to be able to walk on two legs and therefore structurally we've developed a narrower pelvis. This means that we would be able to walk well but wouldn't be able to give birth to babies with significant brain maturity to do things like walking for example, as we don't have the capacity to do this for at least 12-14 months. Other mammals, like horses for example, will have significantly faster brain development and be able to walk within a few hours! As a baby we'll need nurturing but we do have sufficient data innately programmed that tells us we need to smile at our parents in order for us to be fed, picked up and nursed. It's in our neo-natal templates to be able to mimic the faces of our parents in order to get attention. Without this contact and care, babies die despite being well, as previously illustrated.

We then ideally should spend our formative years being cared for by parents or carers during which we learn life lessons, hopefully also in a nurturing environment. Oh but wait a minute! This is the Human Zoo; this is the 21st century we're trying to survive in, not some utopian fantasy after all.

A healthy upbringing will be that there are good things that should happen to a child, that do and there will be good things that should happen that don't. Equally there are bad things that shouldn't happen to kids that don't and there will be bad things that shouldn't happen that actually do.

Isolation, new technologies and the stress response.

If you're in a café right now or a public place, you will see or have seen, couples sitting together not speaking but both looking at their own smart phones together and that's fine. As long as they're both doing this, all will be fine.

What's emerging as a bi-product of all this technological advancement is an interesting phenomenon called proximal abandonment. Imagine you're in a favourite coffee shop and you can see a mother and daughter right in front of you. The mother is busy on an iPad doing her emails and the daughter is sitting looking bored out of her head as if this is a continual transactional pattern that frequently occurs because the mother is present but not really there!

Like me, I'm sure you yourself see this all the time, where people who ideally could be attentive to each other actually aren't because of the interference of technology on social interaction.

We hear of cases of kids committing suicide because of bullying - one example happened less than a week ago at a local train station. The newspapers are awash with cases of child abuse, drug taking, child poverty and such like; again these are cases of things that shouldn't happen but do and things that should happen but don't. As a result of technology being increasingly available, we're seeing this on the increase everywhere. Teenagers spending long hours in their lounges playing the latest PlayStation games, dinner time where families traditionally used to meet to catch up, are fast becoming a thing of the past and now with things like Facebook, we're seeing more and more communication taking place over the internet. It seems to me that technology has made us 'Better connected' and yet despite this, many people feel genuinely isolated and alone. Research of Facebook users more recently has shown that the amount of time spent using this and similar social networks are inversely related to how happy you feel throughout the day.

Healthcare providers AXA in the UK during 2014 conducted a study of 18 to 24 year olds and found that 27% of them reported feeling lonely most of the time, with almost one in four - 24% in the same age group saying that they had no one to talk to almost all the time. So here we are at a time when we've never been so well connected and a significant number of this so called 'connected' generation feel lonely. Amazing to think that at such young ages these people can be feeling lonely as they have so much rich opportunity by embarking on a new career, university, meeting new people, parties with friends, taking gap year trips around the world, meeting new love interests and all the stuff you associate with this age group and a significant number of them tell researchers they're lonely?

These life changing events whilst being new and exciting, can also be perceived in the brain as a threat too. They move away from family, friends, loved ones and familiar places and habits too.

These transitions will often have youngsters who feel unsettled immersing themselves in their studies or workplace to cope or avoid feeling loneliness. This attempt at coping masks the real underlying problems though, which can lead to the vicious circle seeing youngsters becoming even more isolated. According the AXA studies, a quarter of these young respondents also felt they were too busy with work to consider sufficient time with friends and family. This isolation also for a large swathe of this group was apparent where the youngsters were in low paid jobs too. Socialising for example isn't cheap for them and many have to take on part time jobs to fund their lives whilst studying. What was also interesting was the fact that around a quarter of those questioned reported that during the winter they'd restrict their socialising due to the weather and this in itself further adds to the problems they're experiencing.

Loneliness in the young here in the UK and dare I say it, in many other parts of the world, is prevalent and should be taken more seriously as it reveals many hidden phenomena that can return to haunt us in later years too. Additional funding by the government to aid this sector of the population will always be shortcoming during times of austerity and if you are young in this age bracket you will find benefit in getting involved with a local hobby group, take time to reach out to friends and family even if it's just for a chat on the phone or on face time. Even if you're not one of the lonely young ones, you might choose to keep a lookout for signs of loneliness in this age group, perhaps offering to help if they're willing to accept your offer.

Loneliness isn't just making people sick though, it's killing us too. We live in a society where people now judge you not just on your appearance or your money, they judge you on things like how expansive your social network is and of course admitting to being lonely could suggest to others that you're a bit of a loser too. Hard facts these days speak for themselves as studies of the elderly show those who have little or no social interaction are twice as likely to die prematurely and the increased risk of death is comparable to that of smoking and loneliness is considered to be twice as dangerous as obesity. Think back to the SCARF images on page 33 as these were linked to students being ostracised by their friends in a lab experiment and how the brain saw this akin to being physically beaten up.

Social isolation clearly ignites the flight or fight response and longer term impairs immune system functioning which can lead to life threatening conditions like heart disease and type 2 diabetes.

We've all been at parties and meetings where we're surrounded by people and have felt a great sense of being overwhelmed and disconnected as a result of this. There have been many examples of top celebrities who have received much adoration from fans, been invited to great parties, beautiful homes and the most amazing places to holiday and yet feel depressed and isolated. People such as the very brilliant Stephen Fry come to my mind and he's just one of many.

In the realms of human interactions, in order to be socially sated the numbers of people we know isn't a good measure. It is in the quality of our relationships where we gain most benefit. We just need several close people to surround us in our lives who we can mutually depend upon to reach satisfaction. The newspapers here in the UK are awash with obesity and what to do about it, yet another very real killer out there is loneliness. Brigham Young University in the US undertook a meta-analysis study of 70 other studies of over 3.4 million participants and it found that pooling the best studies – those with full adjustment for confounding – showed the increased likelihood of death was 26% for reported loneliness, 29% for social isolation, and 32% for living alone. All were statistically significant increases compared with those reporting less loneliness or social isolation.

Where do other stress traps lie in wait?

'Future Tense' is a remarkable description used by world renowned Futurologist Faith Popcorn on her web site www.faithpopcorn.com She and her consulting team examine the 17 trends that are predicted to drive people's future behaviours for commercial companies. This is how she sums it up; 'Consumers, anxiety-ridden by simultaneous social, economic, political and ethical chaos, find themselves beyond their ability to cope with today or imagine tomorrow.'- Futurologist Faith Popcorn

In this day and age, we unfortunately don't have control of everything because there are many social and economic uncertainties. Control is one of the tenants crucial to our SCARF needs for a happier life experience. What we do have however, is an ability to choose what we pay most attention to. I'd like to illustrate to you some ideas here about what you might like to watch for or be aware of in order to give you a sense of where the stress traps might exist for you in modern life.

Session 4

How things ought to be and how they really are

The way the world ought to be and the way the world actually is can really leave you struggling for a start and is a powerfully toxic trap. For many of us, life can appear unfair, we're many times these days having to do things in our lives and jobs that are beneath us and someone else should be doing and it's just not right that we should suffer this injustice.

Consider the Kenyan baboons that Professor Sapolsky researches. Imagine you're a young, lower hierarchy baboon in the pack and a higher ranking male above you gets beaten up by another competing male over food or territory. The losing baboon then goes down the tree and he slaps a junior baboon in the pack, who is your own father, it's not going to be too long before you yourself get slapped, scratched or worse still, thrown out of the tree! Now that's what I would call real injustice as opposed to what we humans tend to whine about!

Think about a time when someone has whined about their job for example and they say something like, 'This duty shouldn't be for me to undertake, it isn't my job. They don't pay me enough to do it either.' Notice how stressed this has made them become instead of just getting on with it! It's actually not a truth as such that they shouldn't have to deal with this part of the work, it's purely that they have an expectation of the way their job should be and this is really only a thought which is based on their expectations of how the world should be, as opposed to how the world actually is.

If you have expectations of the world that things should be fair, things shouldn't change, the goal posts mustn't be moved and people should be good to their word and we should all have positive experiences, well, you're already misusing your imagination and setting yourself up for a fall. This strategy will leave you continually floundering from one event to another as you get stuck on what's gone wrong and how things should have turned out.

Here's a short exercise you might like to try as a strategy to help overcome expectation mismanagement. The following are a few examples as a starter and you can then add your own:

Example 1

You arrange to meet a friend or a romantic acquaintance for dinner and you get a text message saying that they have been asked to go to dinner with someone else they met at a business meeting and they felt unable to refuse for reasons that aren't divulged in their text.

You might be then tempted to think that this wasn't right, they'd told you that they were going to come along, you'd called them previously and arranged this plus you'd never yourself dream of cancelling out at the last minute unless due to illness. It just isn't right that they chose to go to dinner with someone else as a last minute decision and leave you in the lurch like this! You could have made arrangements if they'd been considerate and called a lot sooner but they didn't. You would have done, of course you would! You shouldn't have to tolerate this let down; after all you'd never do this to them would you?

As you can see this is very much the world as it should be in your mind and how it actually really is. So how do you go about managing this better? First of all you might reframe the outcome and not focus on what has actually taken place.

You might decide to re-write this in your mind by saying, 'Hell it sucks when you get let down but then again, the fact that I chose not to give them a hard time about it could mean that they'll feel a lot warmer toward me for cutting them some slack. Additionally the person who was encouraging them may have been very insistent and it may have been difficult for them, personally, to say no to the demand that they come to dinner. I can re-arrange the meeting with them for another time and sure enough they will come next time.'

Example 2

You wait in for a boiler engineer to come to your house to attend to the repair of your central heating boiler. They told you that they would arrive between 3.00pm and 4.00pm but now it's already 5.15pm and they haven't called to let you know of their whereabouts. When you call them their answer phone immediately cuts in asking you to leave a message.

Apart from the rude message you might be tempted to record, you may also be prone to think that these bloody installers, they're all the same, promising to deliver on time every time and they keep you waiting. You can't even get on with anything just in case they turn up and you miss them. It's just not fair that you pay a lot of money for this stuff and their service is nothing to write home about.

You may decide to reframe this by thinking, well at least I can do some chores or have a coffee and relax, perhaps give them a call in 30 minutes; the chances are that they might just be stuck in traffic and can't make an outgoing call or perhaps they'll arrive within that time and will get on with the work so I can get on with my life. Of course if they don't then I can call them and get a partial refund or discount on the fitting to compensate me for my time.

Example 3

You run a small business that has staff who are responsible for meeting and greeting customers but they aren't always spot on with their customer management and handling. You might be tempted to think that your staff should be capable of doing this themselves, you shouldn't have to be watching them all the time and you certainly shouldn't be expecting to stress about this based on what you pay them, it's just not right! Alternatively you can look at the bigger picture, after all they only had the one unhappy customer and you don't usually get complaints; in fact most, if not all, enjoy using your service. Maybe you could ask one of your other staff to help train their colleague to be better at this; perhaps it was the customer who had an off day themselves?

Maybe you too suffer from the modern day condition of perfectionism. Maybe you'd benefit from looking more closely before jumping to conclusions because the structure of the initial thoughts about the situation aren't ones that you ideally want to have. This is the Ape brain running the game. However, by questioning or reframing the situation, you are engaging the frontal lobes/ frontal cortex with a dash of rational thinking, so by switching your attention you're beginning to de-activate the limbic brain's power over you and allowing both regions of the brain to solve the problem, which is in essence the way emotional intelligence works - you go from having an emotional reaction to thinking more clearly and in a balanced way.

Here's an example of how you might structure your thought process going through each of the 4 steps I outlined in the example below;

1. Situation

You spend time and money on looking after your house. Other family members don't have the same tidiness standards that you expect of them and often leave stuff out all over the place. Them behaving like this is distressing and really unfair in your mind and you tell yourself:

2. I shouldn't have to…

Don't they realise how much of my earnings goes into this house? I shouldn't have to deal with them leaving their stuff lying around - they aren't respectful of me, my efforts and this property.

Here you can begin to question your own emotionally driven propaganda by considering;

3. What's really happening?

Maybe this isn't something that's high on their living agenda, how do others I know live? It's their home too and I should bear that in mind. Is it possible that my standards and expectations are unrealistic?

4. What's possible?

Perhaps I can take a leaf from their book and experiment with not being so tough on myself and others about this. It might be I don't get upset so often, maybe it's just not worth my time and energy worrying about this stuff so much and using this situation for me to learn from.

Now try this exercise for yourself, take a few minutes to think about an experience that has disappointed you and moving through each stage using the same headings to describe and reframe the situation.

Now being a book reader myself, I do know a part of you will be tempted to skip this exercise and go onto the next page. All I would add that whilst this does take a small effort, the rewards of working through this can really pay off dividends well over and above the cost of you investing your time and attention. The act of doing this will produce a great return on your investment and will be worth paying the attention too.

1. Situation

_____

_____

2. I shouldn't have to…

_____

_____

3. What's really happening?

_____

_____

4. What's possible?

_____

_____

Session 5

Stress responses driven by your personality

I often wondered why it was that one person would get stressed terribly about a situation where another wouldn't. Then I became aware of how through your life experiences and upbringing you would focus on what you pay attention to in particular ways that primarily suited your underlying temperament.

To get my point across easily I'd like to share with you the gist of a simple and very brilliant human behaviour model known as DISC personality insights. This is world renowned and has been used to help around 14 million people across the world. It is widely used by the top fortune 500 companies in America and a majority of the UK's FTSE 100 companies too. The original model was conceived back in 1928 by William Marston who originally conceived the lie detector test. He suggested that people's behaviour could be objectively assessed and patterns of behaviour observed scientifically. This is something that had been viewed before by Hippocrates the Greek physician some 2400 years ago. He'd referred to people's behaviours using terminology which appeared to reflect their moods.

These moods were referred to as melancholic, phlegmatic, sanguine and choleric. You can view these styles on youtube.com by typing zack anderson personality into the site's search bar and watching his marvellous enactment of what each personality does when they sit down on a pin placed on a chair. The different reactions are brilliant and illuminating. What is also fun about this video is that you can imagine how you might react too.

The DISC model is a modernised version of this and suggests that behaviours can be divided into 4 particular 'home' styles: Dominant, Influential, Sensitive and Cautious (DISC). Although we're a mix of all four styles, we tend to be one when most comfortable in our environment although we'll switch to one of the other traits if under pressure or as the situation dictates. For example when meeting people you can't be an I style all the time as you'll upset other personality types with your energy and enthusiasm just in the same way as if you were any of the other 3 temperaments, you'll shift to accommodate the circumstances.

The DISC model looks at your energy which describes you as either **outgoing or reserved** in situations and then looks at how you direct this energy and whether you are **task or people** driven in how you expend your efforts.

Here's a visual example of what the DISC model looks like:

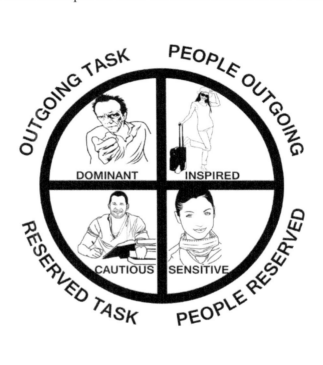

Doesn't it say a thousand words too because as you look at the people images on the next page, I'm sure there will be people with whom you can identify immediately in your life just by looking at this one image. You'll see yourself as being one or probably a mixture of all of these and that's great because you have flexibility in your temperament and mind set. People who tend to be extremes of just one of these behavioural sets struggle most with others in my experience.

Dominant Personality (D) Outgoing and Task Focused

 US business tycoon Donald Trump, has a Dominant tendency, former UK Prime Minister Margaret Thatcher had too. Here in the UK we have well known characters on television like Sir Alan Sugar and Gordon Ramsay who make perfect examples of the Dominant style because they focus on getting stuff done quickly, they'll be movers and shakers and will have a determined attitude to achieve things, so time, money and profitability are high priorities for them. What do you think would be their stress points? Seriously take a moment to think about that before reading on.

If you come up with the following ideas, you'd be about right. The Dominant personality type would freak out about you not doing what you said you were going to do, they'd really become incandescent about you standing around on the job and doing nothing much. This would be stressful in the extreme. They'd worry about losing control and opportunity, their chimp brain really kicks off if they thought they were going to lose money or time as a result of the inactivity of others. They'd struggle to hold their tongue and would be quick to express their displeasure in uncaring tones. If you are a person who tends to have an **outgoing** nature with a **task driven** orientation, think about what in particular stresses you to the max?

The chances are it will be these and other factors but what's so amazing is that you will suffer the same stressors as all the other Dominant types out there in this big wide world. So there's nothing wrong with you, it's just the way you're wired.

Inspired Personality (I) Outgoing and People focused

Inspired people you'll know in the US could be people like the Hollywood actor Will Smith, and familiar people in the UK would include Jonathan Ross, Alan Carr, Lorraine Kelly and Graham Norton who make perfect examples of the Inspired (I) type. Of course what stresses the (I) type will not be the same as what stresses the (D) types. Think for a minute what would stress out an Inspired (I) personality type. They want to be loved; they like fun and hate too much detail about work and projects, unless it's about the people they're working with.

If you had in mind things like others not being enthusiastic for their ideas or projects, people not being fun, friendly or charming you'd be just about right there too. For an Influential style they want not just to be liked, they have to be loved too. They'll want to meet you, ask you how you are and will listen for about 45 seconds. At this point, they'll butt in then spend as much time as possible talking about themselves. If they are on a task, they'll do it but only if there's fun to be had in the work and then they'll also need to know who's involved in the job. If you weren't prepared to listen and be friendly then this would mean that they'd get distressed really quickly. If you're an I style, you'll be thrilled to know that most other I styles like you would get stressed too. It's again all about the way you're wired.

Now bring these two types together and imagine what might happen on a typical day out to the seaside? You have the Dominant character who wants to drive because he or she will get there faster. They will want to set off early so that you can get there on time and have time to spare. Of course on the way you decide to take a visit to the bathroom at a service station. Imagine the reaction of the Dominant personality, they will be not best pleased and they want to know if you'll be able to hold it. Already they're uptight about this and then you decide to stop and talk to someone at the station, maybe get a coffee and a cake too. This will send the Dominant into orbit whilst the Inspired personality will be just happy being out and about. There's no point in sitting around waiting for you to chat and use the toilet because the Dominant personality can always fill up the petrol tank and check emails whilst waiting which will help them remain calm. They've got to be doing something! Finally the Inspired personality type gets back into the car and the Dominant character will then drive quickly as they have to get back past all the drivers they'd overtaken earlier in the morning before you stopped at the services.

Sensitive (S) Personality Types Reserved and people Focused)

Good examples of these people would be Michael J Fox, David Beckham and the talented singer, Susan Boyle. These people don't have to try hard to be liked because they're just easy to get along with and are flexible and willing to do things to help support the needs of others. They want to be supportive of others, like harmony, want people to like them and want others to be kind, faithful and loyal just like them. They love family and connection with others and are happy with things remaining the same in their lives and work. What then do you think though will be the stress points for them? Take a minute or two to consider this before reading on.

If you thought that confrontation would be something they'd prefer to avoid, you'd be absolutely spot on in your thinking; they want everyone to be nice, they want harmony in all things and are likely to withdraw and get emotionally upset if you're not being nice to them or other people who might be involved in the same situation.

One very strong sensitive friend told me that she's so intuitive to how others are feeling that she is aware of other people sitting on the train and their moods and sufferings. She thought that this was overwhelming to say the least but it was part of her mental script. They are not just overly sensitive they do have a tendency to suffer most, usually at the hands of the other 3 main personality blends. They also like to have things as much as possible stay the same and are freaked out by others who want to work with them and introduce sweeping

94

changes to working practices. They will continually allow people to burden them with responsibilities that they aren't convinced they can do anyway, but in order to please others they will accept the tasks often without any protest.

Cautious Personality Types (C) Reserved and Task Focused

As a general rule they don't have to be liked, they just have to be right! People like Microsoft's Bill Gates, John Major, the former conservative prime minister and James Caan the Dragon's Den entrepreneur. They are great people at solving problems, practical, concise and fascinated by details. They live in a literal world and if you tell them you're going to do something you'd better make sure you have done it or there'll be hell to pay. They play fair; they play by the rules and expect everyone else to do so too.

Trouble happens however, when they try to point out that something you said or did wasn't up to their standard or just plain wrong and they can come out appearing negative and critical. They're not meaning to pour water on your fireworks, they just want to help and this is where the problems begin. It's not their intent but the way they try to explain themselves and how they might be perceived that causes problems and stress too. Think about what will get the Cautious personality types stressed?

If you came up with people, in particular the (I) styles who talk lots but don't say much you'd be right, as the Cautious don't like having conversations with them; they never ever keep to the point. Additionally if you tell a C type you're going to meet them at 10.00am you'd better be on time as they will have arrived at 09.50am and they find lateness in others really difficult to come to terms with. That stress pales into insignificance if any project you're working on isn't keeping to plan, changes suddenly without warning, or worse still there's not even one been made yet prior to the project beginning.

At work you will know if you are dealing with a (C) personality if they like correcting spelling mistakes made by other people, if you write a memo to them, be sure to spell-check your correspondence as spelling mistakes will make them go crazy. Of course these stressors may be particular to the Cautious (C) type but they aren't necessarily stress inducers for the other personality types.

When I first came across these ideas it was through a brilliant man called Dr Robert A Rohm and he tells a story in one of his instructional videos of when he and his mother go to see an eye surgeon at Emory University Hospital in Atlanta. His mother is a Sensitive (S) type personality and he tells her that the surgeon is a Cautious (C) type personality and that he's there to fix her eye and she shouldn't expect the surgeon to want to get to know her.

In the movie clip he then explains that the eye surgeon comes in after a 30 minute wait and simply acknowledges Mrs Rohm and invites her to sit in front of an eye diagnostic machine into which he peers. He makes a few notes, asks her to look left and then look right before telling her that he wants to do surgery early next week due to cataracts, and then quickly leaves the room.

The surgery takes place and the doctor returns to Mrs Rohm's bedside and he examines his handy work. They remove the bandages from Mrs Rohm's face and she tells them that this is the best she's been able to see for nearly 80 years. With that, the Doctor thanks Mrs Rohm for the compliment and then leaves to get on with his round and professional duties elsewhere.

Dr Rohm then goes on to explain that Mrs Rohm would have wanted to get to know that doctor, being a Sensitive (S) type but the Doctor, being a Cautious (C) type would have been happier if they'd delivered her eye balls in a jar. It would have been so easy to misrepresent her expectations of what should have happened in this situation but for Robert Rohm's expert knowledge in behavioural profiling. This shortfall in expectations would almost certainly have caused a great deal of resentment from the Sensitive (S) type whereas the Cautious (C) type clinician was just doing the job, to a very high standard clinically but perhaps not to the standard she wanted due to misrepresented expectations caused by her temperamental focus.

As you can see, this brief insight into personality profiling shows that much of what unconsciously stresses us is often caused by our personal temperament and how the world should actually be, based on our own personal behavioural biases. If you'd like to see the video I described and more you can visit youtube.com and type in 'Our Personalities Affect Everything We Do' - Robert Rohm, PhD (DISC expert) Dr Robert A Rohm and you'll get around 15-20 short movie videos telling you a whole range of fantastic stories which will help bring the DISC model to life.

Additionally you might consider what for your personality style you think your stress triggers are likely to be and consider how you can counter these more effectively by the way you expect life to be. (D) Dominant types should maybe consider easing up on themselves about having to be in charge of everything and being the one who wins at everything. (I) Inspired styles might want to consider not worrying so much about what everyone else thinks about them and being much better organised in their lives.

(S) Sensitive types will do well to say no from time to time because it doesn't make you a bad person to say no, it shows you are considerate to yourself as much as others too. Finally the (C) types might ease off on their unrealistic expectations of themselves and others that things have to be perfect and maybe they should just try hanging out a little more and certainly trying to be friendly too.

If you are interested in learning more about this you can also attend one of my lectures on this topic. Details of these talks can be found at www.affinitytraining.org

Getting the message?

I'm suggesting that managing your thinking better is likely to reduce your stress response activation but it's something that isn't abstract, it's actually something to take action on now, please don't wait for retirement – please, please don't wait till your happier or you have that new job you dream about or meet the ideal partner to spend your life with, you'll get better if you begin now. Go from fight or flight to a get up and go philosophy when managing your thinking because the way you handle stress today will affect you tomorrow and in the years to come and it's clear that the long term effects of stress can have significant, even life or death consequences.

In truth, I'm not suggesting that people repeatedly stressed are killed by stress; I'm suggesting that the stress response repeatedly firing off, sometimes many times a day causes the human immune system over time to be less effective which then results in humans being more susceptible to infections and disease which cause death!

Knowing that the stress doesn't kill you but affects a whole range of things like the immune system can be a real eye opener for people because what is suggested now is that somewhere between the two issues of stress and its link to disease is healing too.

Where healing lies, to my mind, there is hope! I don't mean sudden massive miracle healing episodes, where people have jumped up proclaiming like Lazarus, that they are able to rise from death. I mean that you can also, with attention direction, begin to train your thinking in better, more productive ways. Healing takes place in so many ways and at so many levels. Think for a moment about someone receiving hospitalised palliative care and nearing death. They can be feeling nauseous and absolutely terrible one day and a little better the next! That's the healing I mean.

On the other end of the spectrum, you can wake and think, 'Oh God, it's Monday,' only to find around 11.00am the very same morning, that you've chatted to a friend and found yourself in a better mood - well that's what I refer to as healing, because both are valid life experiences where you've managed to feel better and therefore the spectrum of healing to which I am referring can be wide and varied from a physical and psychological level too.

We all clearly have a personal relationship with stress and it affects us all in different ways and at so many levels. If left unchecked, it can become a raging inferno, bedevilling our minds, igniting our nights and upsetting our balance and equilibrium. It's clearly also important to know that it's something you have to do something about now!

Becoming increasingly positive

One day the devil decided to sell some of his tools - these lethal weapons include lies, deception, hatred and a whole host of other items. In the corner however, he had one item that was priced higher than any other. When asked why this tool was nearly 4 times the price of all the other tools put together (especially as it looked so worn and used), the devil replied, 'It's my favourite tool, it works better than all the tools I have and it works every time and

It's called discouragement and best of all it gets them every time.'

Each and every day we can face situations and events that provide plenty of this. Like me I am sure you'd agree that it's so easy to be discouraged, especially when things don't go the way you planned. Truthfully though, there are few things in a busy working day that actually ever go exactly the way you planned or hoped for. Life is more a journey than it is an actual destination. You have to be really careful not to allow discouragement to trip you up and keep you from getting to your desired destination or becoming the sort of person you think you were designed to be.

So how can you turn this around and remain buoyant despite constant opportunities for discouragement? I have a few ideas that you may enjoy from here on in to manage and exercise your monkey mind.

Session 6

Training ideas and exercises to be more optimistic

This last section of the book is to bring to your attention to some of the neatest ideas I have seen from the leading lights in the field of positive psychology that are easy to do, effective and work fast. This means that you won't have to do so much thinking that it hurts and you turn this book into what I call 'Brain porn.' The meaning of this phrase is that psychology books will contain exercises that are often just too hard to do. It's not that they're actually in reality really, really hard, it's just that our human, overstressed and attention split brains will perceive the exercises in this way.

What then happens is that you tell yourself that this is something that looks good but I will come back to it. What that really is saying is that you never will! It requires too much attention and your cingulate anterior cortex goes into 'Help I'm being attacked mode,' firing off and you get an emotional overload shutting down motivation, causing you to skip an exercise that can have amazing effects if you actually did do it and you're then prone unconsciously to be forever reading book after book hoping one day that you will change. How can this happen though if you continue to do the same thing time and time again, you'll just get the same result as you've always gotten. So here goes, some exercises to tax your brain, but not so much that it hurts!

Psychology Professor, Barbara Fredrickson examined positivity in team behaviour and over a 4 week period had participants record their positive and negative emotions. What they found from this was those who had an equal ratio of 1 negative and 1 positive emotion had no better sense of well-being than those who were predominantly negative. Even more surprising was her discovery that those who had 2 positive emotions to 1 negative emotion were little or even no happier than those whose negative emotions' ratio exceeded the positive ones. Once positive emotions however were 3 to 1 negative emotion - that is for every three instances of feeling gratitude, interest or contentment, they experienced only one instance of anger, guilt or embarrassment, these subjects genuinely flourished in their workplaces. Clearly positive forces and thoughts give us levity which lifts you skyward whereas gravity in the form of negative emotions keeps you grounded, pulling you earthward toward reality.

What may be a great idea to start with is to go to Barbra Fredrickson's web page http://positivityratio.com/ and take her positivity test, you can complete this in a little under 2 or 3 minutes and this will yield your current positivity ratio. Then you can go ahead and like me establish an account that will allow you to track your ratio over time. Fredrickson indicated that the ten positive emotions could be joy, gratitude, serenity, interest, hope, pride, amusement, inspiration, awe and love. Take two minutes to write these down and try each day to find opportunities where one or two these can be experienced. It's invigorating to see your positivity levels rise but don't take my word for it, try this for yourself!

Have a word with yourself…

Ever notice the fact that the way you think is often represented by language and self-talk? In other words we tell ourselves stories about the way things happen in life. You see an event occurring in front of you and it's entirely possible someone else seeing the same event would have a different perspective.

If you are human, you will have had set backs in your life, we all have and these will continue to challenge us day in and day out, moment by moment. It's not the fact that we have setbacks that's the problem. It's about how we react to them in the way we do that makes all the difference.

Something happens at your workplace to you or another colleague that you don't think is very nice; let's for example say that your boss gives your colleague a real dressing down for their work standard or conduct. You're there in the room when this takes place and the scene gets ugly with both people ending up arguing. It shouldn't happen but it does –

remember these thing go on and on throughout life and not just childhood!

The chances are that like most human beings you will go through a process of examining this situation in your own mind. Here's an interesting Neuro Linguistic Programming formula that many humans tend to use to examine this situation in their mind:

Event + Reaction = Outcome

We'll often begin focussing on what actually happened i.e. **The Event**

... You might say to yourself something along the lines of, 'It was awful of him to speak to Jenny in that way, it wasn't really even her fault that the delivery arrived late and besides if he did have a grievance then surely he should have done this in private and not dragged us in to the situation too.'

As you now know, the brain is wired more toward the threat than the reward and therefore many people will spend their time initially replaying the event back to themselves over and over. Of course as you now know we're addicted to this and just the act of replaying this time and time again in our mind will set off an internalised threat response i.e. **The Reaction...** Let's of course not forget that the same thing could happen to you the next time. Before you know it, the body has gone off into an internal fight or flight response, even though the event occurred several hours earlier and you're now at home talking to a friend.

Of course you can now also begin to see that these two powerful factors, **Event** plus **Reaction** will then begin to colour how you see the **Outcome** itself. 'It was horrible, the boss was a real monster, talking to Jenny that way and what if this happened to me too, how would I react?' All this replaying of the **Event** mixed with the **Reaction** will prime the unconscious limbic system to be more aware of threats like your boss, just in case he decided to kick off at you too. Of course your boss may be happy with your work and has no beef with you and yet your limbic chimp brain will nevertheless encourage you to remain on alert status just in case. In other words your perception of the **Outcome** has changed too because you're likely to be more fearful of reprisals occurring against you in the future.

It's amazing that the very moment you have a negative thought, primal regions of your brain activate and areas in your brain linked to motivation, imagination and creativity shut down. Dendrons that connect and transmit electrical activity between neurons in the brain, quite literally explode!

So the consequences of a negative neural activation are real but does the same apply to the thought itself? Does having a thought make it reality? Do you have to believe your own propaganda or is it just hype driven by the chimp brain?

The brain has a role to activate for safety which is why people, when faced with new learnings or the idea of doing something challenging will experience emotional strain. This is because the brain will enlist information often in the format of past failures and paying attention to your internal dialogue using words associated with negatives produce cortisol, however if you pay attention to more optimistic language patterns in your head, this can produce endogenous hormones such as dopamine which is associated with curiosity and interest as well as opiate-like substances such as endorphins which are shown to even illicit a placebo-like effect. When the moments you feel under pressure aren't as bad as they might appear, it is because you are able to explain the event to yourself in a more optimistic way than just being stuck in the **Event +Response = Outcome.** The next question is how do you go about making this happen?

Measuring optimism and examining your personal explanatory style

Who do you know in your life that when plans and arrangements don't go to plan, they simply go into meltdown, become stressed and allow the event and its consequences to ruin their day, week, month, year or life?

We're all prone to setbacks and disappointments but I am referring to someone you'll know has their life repeatedly knocked out of kilter and each time it takes them longer to recover until one day they finally won't.

This is referred to as 'Learned helplessness' and it occurs in humans and animals confronted by a situation where they believe the situation is hopeless and can't be made better despite environmental cues existing that suggest hope is abundant.

Try typing pike syndrome into youtube.com and you can watch an amazing 1970s experiment about how a pike in a large fish tank attacks a small shoal of Minos, its favourite dish. Only trouble is that the Minos are inside a clear jar inserted into the tank, which means that the pike keeps banging up against this, the resulting actions of the Minos is also interesting because they scatter. This continual action of bashing against the jar means pain for the pike and it's going to get worse unless he stops bashing his face against it and sure enough he does.

At this point the scientists reintroduce the Minos back into the main body of the tank by removing the open bottom jar in which the Minos were previously swimming; the Minos swim freely around the pike and now the pike has become conditioned by learned helplessness, that to try and attack the Minos will result in pain, so much so that it doesn't even bother to try and the result is that it starves, despite there being an abundance of its favourite dietary dish, Minos. They're swimming literally within centimetres of its mouth toward the end of the experiment and it gives up and doesn't even try to catch them and finally starves. Like I said, it's something that needs to be seen to be believed!

Martin Selligman is a Professor of Psychology at the University of Pennsylvania; he's also the leading light in helping people become happier in their lives and work. You can visit the web site *tedtalk.com* and type in the new era of positive psychology. In this talk he discusses his views on this topic which are certainly illuminating.

Selligman is widely acknowledged as the grandfather of positive psychology and his work in the last 30 years has helped transform the way psychology works to examine the mind not just from a disease model perspective but also to examine happiness and optimism with just as much intensity. This means that people are much more empowered to help themselves with the right kind of understanding and insights becoming increasingly available to everyone.

His early work in the 70's was on dogs and he was able to demonstrate that they experienced degrees of helplessness in laboratory conditions, where they were being exposed to electrical shocks and some chose to simply give up trying to escape from the situation. It wasn't too long as you might imagine that his attention began to turn toward humans and sure enough he found that they too also exhibited similar patterns of behaviour.

Selligman noticed that human beings exhibited an 'explanatory style,' a way that they talk to themselves about their experience of events. Selligman discovered that an individual's depressive episodes tended to be more frequent, deeper and longer lasting if they had a fatalistic explanatory style and didn't feel that they had control over situations. Even when conditions returned to normal, the individuals involved in Selligman's experiments who were stripped of control continued to do nothing despite being able to move away from pain, they remained in situations during the experiments which saw them continuing their discomfort.

Optimists on the other hand were more likely to succeed because they see a set-back as a learning experience, an unfortunate incident which will enable them to be better at doing the same things in the future. Therefore among optimists, depressive episode frequency rates were lower, the length of the episodes were considerably shorter and the individuals with the optimistic mind-set appeared to recover much more quickly, as they were better able to review the events in their mind. All this appears to be down to factors surrounding our perception of **permanence, personalisation** and **pervasiveness** and how we attach these to the meanings of the events to ourselves.

Let's say we have an event like a driving test; there are two outcomes, one being that you fail and the other is that you pass. Scenario 1: The driving test failure - many of us have got the T shirt for this one, I passed after 5 attempts! A candidate who tends to see the world from a gloomy and fatalistic point of view, might say to themselves, 'Failed again huh! What was I thinking? I knew I'd never pass my test...This isn't the first time and I need to get this before my job interview otherwise I can't possibly apply. What's the use in trying.' You can see that the person who failed their test appeared to almost own the failure, so it was **personalised** toward them. They also then told themselves they knew they'd never pass and here again we have a toward **permanence** aspect which is finally supported by the fact that this isn't the first time they failed so the toward momentum is about **pervasiveness.** The event affects all parts of their life as they can't get a job without passing first.

If however we were to re-run this scenario again but this time the person failing the driving test has a more optimistic bent, he may say something to himself that's entirely different, maybe something like, 'The examiner, what an idiot, he had not a clue about how to conduct a test and I'd have done fine if the driver of that car hadn't pulled out until after I passed the corner. Still I can always re-apply for a short term cancellation test, there must be some going that I could do later in the month.' Notice now how the explanation of the optimist is entirely different despite the set-back of failing the test. He's **personalised** the event away from himself by blaming the examiner for being unable to do his job and the other driver for pulling out too soon. Then he has moved the **permanence** of the event away by suggesting that he will attempt to get another test if it's available soon and judging by the mental response in his head, he's not going to let this affect other parts of his life which is how he sees this in **pervasiveness** terms. It's not the end of the world!

Scenario 2: The driving test success! Again many people will pass their driving tests and it's down to the way they explain this to themselves that makes all the difference. So we now have a positive outcome and you'd think even the most negative person would see this in a good light. Don't be so sure... The more fatalistic explanatory style might be along the lines of, 'I passed the test, at last but then again I was lucky. He didn't spend too much time asking me about the Highway Code rules and the area I did my 3 point turn in was much bigger than I imagined and had practiced for...I was lucky. Now I have to go out and find insurance for the next 12 months and insurance these days is so expensive and will only be set to rise if I crash or worse still I get hit by an uninsured driver.'

In the case of the more optimistic candidate, they may tell themselves something like, 'I passed my test...I knew I could, there were one or two moments I was worried but I managed to keep it together. I'm good at passing tests generally and I can get on with other stuff now'. As you can see, this candidate has **personalised** the success of the event toward himself by thinking he's good at passing tests. They now attribute the success to the **permanence** aspect of their life by already being ready to move on in life, now that they have passed the test itself.

Scenario 3: The date's gone wrong and we've all had them! Imagine you're out on a date to meet a perspective new partner who you met on a dating website. The initial contact was good and you were doing well on the dating site's complimentary messenger service. It's off to a good start but when you meet up for a coffee after about 45 minutes you both dry up and the promise of things continuing further rapidly goes downhill. You both decide to call it an early night, making an excuse that you have work the next day and not wanting to appear rude, you leave disappointed at the outcome.

The more fatalistic thought process might be, 'Oh that didn't go well, she wasn't impressed by my conversation and come to think of it, this isn't the first time something like this has gone wrong. I wish I was smarter and wittier and that I could keep their attention on me going for longer and more often. This dating lark is so hit and miss I don't like the uncertainty.'

Dissecting this statement you can see that the **personalisation** of this unfortunate event is attributed toward the person thinking that they weren't witty enough to hold the attention of the partner. Added to this was also that the event was becoming increasingly **permanent** as this wasn't the first time that this had occurred.

In the mind of a more optimistic character, the explanatory style of this unfortunate event might have been along the lines of, 'Oh that didn't go well, maybe she was tired and come to think of it I probably wasn't on my best form either. I will see what she says when she next posts me after all; you can't guarantee the outcomes from these sorts of things. It'll be her loss if she doesn't call, I am sure it won't be long before I meet a few other girls, maybe I should call a few friends and find out if they have any parties they're going to over the weekend.'

As you'll see there is still **personalisation** of the event, however this is an 'away from' style because the thought process suggests that they were both tired and these things are hit and miss. The **permanence** of this event is still apparent but in an 'away from', short term format. He's already considering the possibility of meeting other people later at the weekend which means the **pervasiveness** is suggesting very little of his life is being affected by this incident. He's open minded to the possibility that she could call back, the other person might have really been tired as they'd said on the date when they were together.

Scenario 4: What if the date had gone well though, and you'd both hit it off together, how would the explanatory styles compare here?

The fatalist might have talked to themselves about the surprise that this had gone so well. 'I didn't think she'd be interested because the last few dates I've been out on were disasters. It's a good job she didn't ask me about my previous girlfriends on this occasion because she'd soon realise that I have emotional baggage that she may not like. I hope the next date goes well, I hope she likes to go out for dinner or maybe she'd prefer a movie or a walk in the park.' Trouble is, I don't know which she'll prefer and I wouldn't like to get it wrong. I hope she likes me because nice girls like this aren't easy to find.'

Despite the relative success enjoyed on the date, the fatalist thinking style will **personalise** the success of the date away from themselves and onto external events. 'The date went well but that was because she didn't ask me about previous girlfriends'. Then he's added pervasiveness and permanence to the mix when talking about previous dates all being disasters which of course they may not have been but this is indeed the black and white thinking nature of those with the fatalist mind-set.

The optimist might say, 'What a lovely girl, she was so nice but come to think of it I'm one hell of a catch too. Where can we go next time? We could try a few places and see which we both like. There's plenty of choice and who knows we might hit it off again!' The optimist has attributed the success of the date or its **personalisation** toward himself, after all he believes himself to be, 'One hell of a catch' and now he's applying some variations of **permanence** in talking himself into a positive outcome for the next date, whereas by contrast the fatalist was looking at all the obstacles and why the date might fail.

So what are the ways you can improve your optimism levels?

I would recommend that you test your own personal optimism levels using the University of Pennsylvania optimism test which measures your optimism levels about the future and it's designed by Selligman. It's free and accurate in my experience. You can go back from time to time to test yourself on things like how you rate for attributional facts like Pervasiveness-for Good Events;

Permanence- for Good Events; Pervasiveness-for Bad Events; Permanence-for Bad Events and Hopefulness.

Secondly you might choose to work on your explanatory script by questioning your thinking, much in the same way a top legal barrister would question a defendant or witness in the courtroom. You can use this clever and easy to learn method devised by Selligman and his team - it's referred to as the A,B,C,D, E model:

(A) Activating event - The moment a perceived pressure or setback comes directly into your conscious awareness. These aren't difficult to come up with as we're surrounded by them each and every day. So to illustrate, here's a recent example that occurred for me. Of course

110

you might have a different take on this but it's for illustrative purposes to demonstrate how to do this.

I received an email from a customer to inform me that due to operational circumstances he would be unable to book me and couldn't envisage doing so for at least another 6 months. It was disappointing as he'd a day or two before told me he would be doing so and appeared really interested too.

(B) Belief - Usually the first thing that hits you by way of an explanatory style. The first thought that came to my mind was, 'What a fucking thing to happen, that's going to cost me £600 minimum and I hate things like this, plus it's by no means the first time this has happened. I could well do without this stuff. Fuck it what an arse this business can be!'

(C) Consequence - This is how the event makes you feel. I was initially disappointed and slightly saddened but that was about all. Truthfully though, before I discovered this A,B,C,D,E method it would have been full on seething resentment, disgust, outrage and the hurt surrounded by the bloody unfairness of it all and why does it happen to me! That has as you can see changed my own explanatory style and reactions with practice and application of Selligman's system, which is why I encourage you to try this for size! I like things that actually do work and make your recovery better and faster.

(D) Disputation - This is how you begin to question and reframe the event and surrounding circumstances rather than allowing the propaganda of your chimp/limbic brain run riot by replaying the event over and over, fuelling the fires, affecting the way you perceive the outcome.

I recall thinking, 'It's a shame that this has happened, I would like to avoid these things but sometimes they're just out of my control to command. It doesn't happen that much these days either.' I also thought about the fact that despite previous cancellations from other customers, they always came back and re-booked again for more training. I had only had one booking cancelled this year so far but in 2010 I had 22 cancellations! Things were definitely on the up by comparison and the odd cancellation was part of the process. 'I'll just diary his details in my Outlook program and get back to him again in six months when he'll probably have the budget available.'

(E) Energiser - This is simply how thinking differently or reframing the event can make you feel differently and what you can learn from being more in control about handling the set back itself.

I was pleased with how little emotional arousal I had gone through about receiving this note from my customer. I was also pleased about the fact that the customer was thankful of my willingness to accommodate a change of his plans. I then made an effort to get on with some other things that morning but guess what happened next. Another customer drops me a quick note following my most recent email campaign to let me know that he now wanted to make a booking and could I let him have dates for this.

Now I realise that I may well have received his booking nevertheless but going through the process this way reminded me that I am getting better at handling this type of stuff as well.

So what you might like to do now is think about the event or setback that's been most recent.

(A) Activating Event - Just write it down with the briefest of information because chances are you will remember the details all too well, especially if you've normally been used to running them over and over! Give it a scoring rating too on a scale of 1-10 with 1 being not at all painful or emotional and 10 representing a complete emotional hi-jack where you experienced a pike syndrome moment! Helpless and unable to change your circumstances.

(B) Belief - What was the first thought that came into your mind, what did you actually say to yourself? Use expletives as much as you like, they really do help with this, I've found.

(C) Consequence - How did this make you feel in the moment? Angry, resentful, saddened, ashamed, outraged, hurt are often good words to start with.

(D) Disputation - The key here is to think about what evidence there is that exists to counter your emotional propaganda and whether or not it's real.

Go from pain to positive

Using solution-focused questions in these situations too is a good approach to amplify the use of the A.B.C.D.E. technique

Do events happen like this all the time, probably not!

Will this go on forever? Most unlikely but just check to make sure nonetheless.

Does this really, really happen all the time?

Have things like this happened before and how did you get past them?

How will the situation look different in one day, one week, one month or one year from now?

What will it be like for you to look back at this event in six months and feel confused as to why it should have bothered you so much?

What other possibilities exist following the set back?

Could there have been factors pressuring down on the other parties involved that might not exist in a few months that would allow for a different outcome?

Is the other party's point of view actually really factual or just an opinion based on their warped views of how the world should work?

Is it possible that they may be wrong? After all there's no point in both of you being wrong about the same thing!

What's the worst possible thing that could happen as a result of this situation? What's the best possible thing that could happen and what's most likely to happen?

What would a friend of yours tell you to do about this situation that is more productive than the outcomes you have made up in your head?

If you were to wave a magic wand over the situation and everything suddenly became better, what would change and how would you act differently?

What can I learn from this event that I can take into the future? Remember that the amygdala will scan and recall this change of reference which is far better than just being an effect of outside circumstances, so that when faced with the same situation again or faced with one similar will mean it reacts more positively later as this now has a new patterned match strategy.

(E) Energizer - As you have gone through the questions I would like you to notice how you have emotionally shifted your perception of the event in just a few short minutes. What is the new grading you would give this reframed version in your mind between 1-10? How much has the intensity of the feeling reduced? Usually by around 25% most people report even from feeling stressed out in less than 10 minutes is pretty cool.

Think about this, you haven't fundamentally changed any of the circumstances surrounding the event but you have changed how your brain remembers the event which in turn teaches your body new insights to feel more comfortable about how you remember the event. Oh the wonders of neuroplasticity never fail to amaze me!

What is so good about this exercise is that you can do this either during the stressful moment or after. I have always found this to be a trusted old faithful that has helped me and many clients. You needn't take my word for it, it's something that Selligman conceived of which I am thankful for in my life and if you choose to use it, you will be too but it does take repeated persistence in the way you pay attention.

Other simple techniques for managing your mind that prove helpful take no time at all, so here's a great one to try.

Try a new morning routine

Most people wake up first thing in the morning and if, you're like most people you'll probably have waking thoughts which will be focused on what I refer to as a 'lack of something.' This can be a lack of time to get to work, lack of sleep, lack of a weekend, lack of money for what you do, a lack of resources, a lack of years that you have to live or a lack of the things you have done in life as well as a lack of other people who can help you or a lack of people who understand how much stress your life is under and they make demands of you. There's a lack of time to get to work, there's a lack of seats on the train and you've paid a fortune for the season ticket too. Notice the limbic brain kicking in and your cingulate anterior cortex about how unfair this is and it's galling to be robbed by overpaid train companies who don't care or relate to you and when you do finally get to work, minus delays and overcrowding, there's always a lack of time to get things done and that's before you've even actually opened your emails for the day!

Then when you start reading the emails, you realize there are dozens that need your attention and suddenly your amygdala jumps in and kicks your left pre-frontal cortex into touch. This feels like a heart sink moment you wish you were anywhere else but here. You will now fully appreciate that your central nervous system is in full flight or fight mode and you're off on one. Oh hang on, there aren't even any lions about! That's because there doesn't even need to be. You're already in the Human Zoo - the next question is, do you want to thrive rather than survive?

There's a nice practical way you can help yourself which was highlighted by Dr Heidi Hannah of the American Institute for Stress. She suggests that a great way to start your day is to wake first thing and write a list of 10 things you're grateful for and that you appreciate about your life.

Additionally reflecting back on your previous day and noting down too what has gone well is also very helpful as your experiences of life after a good night's sleep are never actually as good or as bad as you might think they were at the time they occurred.

This isn't the easiest thing to do especially first thing or even when you first start trying to do it however, the brain can learn new tricks fairly quickly. Over time it is something that comes easier and faster and if you stick to it , by day 30 you'll find the very way in which you pay attention will have changed too.

Combating fear, stress and worry...final ideas!

According to Dr Travis Bradberry, author of Emotional Intelligence 2.0, there tend to be two kinds of people when it comes to managing stress. The first believe they can make things happen in their lives and the others are more fatalistic by thinking that life happens to them and there's little they can do to change this.

Research by Tim Judge, Psychologist at Florida University shows that people in the first category tend to do better in life, make more money, enjoy better health, live longer, adjust better to change and the speed at which it happens. They are confident and end up doing better on nearly every measure of working performance.

If you are already one of these top performing people, congratulations! Just in case you're not and that's why you're probably reading this book, you might enjoy reading some simple tips to up your game.

Recognise success or failure are a continuum of scales and nothing more...

When you're enjoying personal success, you can begin to believe that the world is at your feet. Those who do really well, recognise that when the going in life gets tough, they don't lose perspective and become overwhelmed. Successful people will feel stress and anxiety in adversity. Their anxiety is used to fuel determination and passion as opposed to pity and despair.

Anxiety is there to help us make a change, it's our unconscious mind telling us that there needs to be action taken to dispel or alleviate the uncertainty we face. Managing this for what it really is as opposed to succumbing to the pike syndrome or repeated learned helplessness is the key.

If we can send people into space why can't we manage our emotions?

Research from Yale has shown that when we're experiencing high state stress responses, entire areas of our brain shut down, also known as 'emotional hi-jacking.' This reduces our ability to regulate self-control and clarity of mind. This simply means that you're then likely to struggle at times of stress and also be more likely to get into situations with greater frequency.

Change happens so be prepared in advance

Life has ebbs and flows, it has its sweet ups and terrifying downs. The major factor at play is that you believe that you are capable of dealing with changes and something positive will come from it.

I'm not good at anticipating change myself but have found great help in setting a time, once a week, for no more than 10 minutes, to listing the possible changes that might occur in my business or personal life. It has opened my mind and has sharpened me to be more alert for evidence of forthcoming change.

Og Mandino the philosopher said, 'My life has been filled with worry, most of which never happened.' The lesson here for you is that most of what you write down will not actually come to pass but the practice of preparing and listing these fears will give your unconscious commands to handle better the changes that actually do.

Finally when you have listed the predicted changes, instead of taking time to think about how limited and powerless you might be to influence the changes, begin focusing on what abundances of control you can experience in light of the changes. Jot down all the positive ways in which you can take action and you'll be surprised how much actual real control you really do have on your side.

This exercise once a week for 10 minutes will build self-belief because doing this will reduce the fight or flight response associated with cortisol and adrenalin. This is replaced by amazing chemical compounds such as dopamine which promotes interest, curiosity and intrigue as well as endorphins that heal pain and promote a healthy outlook and make you feel more optimistic.

Remove the CRAP from your mind

Another exercise that you'll enjoy very much is the act of getting stuff that's in your head out and onto paper. I did this in the last few days for the third time, before actually writing this section of the book. It was quick, easy to do and has had super-fast ongoing results which is why I felt compelled to let you know about it. This idea is presented by Dr Mark Waldman, who is one of the world's leading experts on communication, spirituality and the brain. He is on the faculty at Loyola Marymount University's College of Business and the Holmes Institute. It's called the 'CRAP board' which is a nice acronym for **conflicts, resistance, anxieties and problems** (CRAP). He suggests that the brain is more likely to look at problems over any solutions about a situation. The brain ruminates so much about all this that we become addicted by habituation to the familiarity of it all and it keeps flagging up the problems throughout our waking hours if they're not being dealt with or acted upon.

That's because the brain is a hard drive where the problems get stored for retrieval. Waldman recommends that you take a single page of paper and actually write down a list of all the conflicts, resistances, anxieties and problems that you're having, make the list long as you can too - mine was 25 CRAPS in total!

The list started with me not ever finishing this book, the book being a disaster and not being liked, me not being a nice enough father to my daughter and not being liked by other people and this list goes on and on and so hopefully   yours too will prove to be lengthy one.

According to Waldman, this makes the paper similar to a secondary hard drive where you can store the information and get it out of your brain. The next stage - and this is surprisingly easy - is just to sit back, take slow deep breaths, watch the paper, read this list, relax and let it wash over you for several minutes.

What you'll find, as I did, is how quickly this causes you to become calm. Despite the fears being listed right there in front of you, your mind just lets them go onto the paper. It is important to keep this list on your desktop or at least visible so your brain or the limbic region of it at least can retain a psychological connection to it. Having them there in front of you, in plain sight will remind you not to reload this detail back into your main consciousness circuitry. I have myself found this to be the simplest of all the exercises and have remained calm and disassociated from my worry for several weeks already and yet I still know at one level, that they're still there and yet I have surprisingly remained un-plagued by them since doing the exercise the first time round.

On this occasion the list was actually longer but several of the things I had been worrying about previously on my list were no longer applicable and when I compared both lists I found myself confused as to why I had bothered even worrying about some of the original things in the first place.

In my therapeutic experiences, symptom utilisation strategies just like this work brilliantly well when utilised in a reframe and confusion like this is never a bad thing as your focus will, like mine, move in emphasis from worrying about something troubling to wondering why you've ever bothered worrying about it at all. Even more wonderful is that there have been no instrumental outside changes that have influenced the situation in any way but your brain has gently allowed itself to reframe the stimulus.

Since writing this part I have also submitted to well over 100 other interested readers of my newsletters this exercise and they found that results broadly speaking were just as effective so it's absolutely worth doing.

Dissolving problem based thinking

Whilst removing CRAP, you might want to also eradicate the word **'but'** from your thinking mechanisms.

The way you hold on to a problem is reflected in the use of language in your own mind - think back to the exercise Michael Moseley, the BBC Science correspondent did with words on fridge magnets earlier on in this book. Just in case you skipped looking at the video, he ran experiments on students at University College London. The students in the first group were asked to arrange words associated with old age, words like, 'old, faithful, loyal and frail' and interestingly enough, all the students after doing the exercise left the room and walked down the corridor slower than when they came in. One student was nearly 30% slower following the experiment.

Then the second group were brought in and again sorted fridge magnet words into sentences but this time the words were associated with youthfulness and vitality. This time they left the room much quicker, in fact one lady who wasn't very slim appeared to bound down the corridor by comparison to her entry. So if words on a fridge magnet can make you go faster or slower, then what can words used inside of your head do too?

Read this sentence:

'I would love to lose weight, get slimmer **but** I don't have time to go to the gym after work.' What does this statement really appear to be saying to you?

The chances are you're thinking that there is a restriction in the other person's mind to actually losing weight.

Now re-read the next sentence:

'I would love to lose weight, get slimmer **and** I have no time to go to the gym after work. How has this statement changed now for you? What does it appear to be saying.

Now add the word '**so**…'

'I would love to lose weight, get slimmer **and** I have no time to go to the gym after work, **so**….'

What comes to your mind next? Notice how your mind sets to the task of now trying to think about what you're going to do to manage the 'no time excuse' with a better, more productive strategy.

'I would love to lose weight, get slimmer **and** I have no time to go to the gym after work, so….I will make sure that I leave work earlier to avoid the traffic and get to the gym.'

Notice how much more solution-oriented this statement makes you feel. No longer is the word **'but'** getting in the way and justifying what is often a lame excuse as a pseudo-rationalisation for remaining complacent and stuck where you are. I wonder how many times do you fall victim to this? Wouldn't now reading this book be a great time to dispel this unhelpful piece of mental software?

Take a piece of paper and write down something you would like to do or improve upon. Here's an example to get you started.

'I want to pass my work proficiency examination **but** I am worried that I can't concentrate on this when I sit down to do the revision in the evening.' Replace the word 'but' by adding **'and'** and **'so.'**

'I want to pass my work proficiency examination **and** I am worried that I can't concentrate on this when I sit down to do the revision in the evening, **so**…I will not try to study all at once like I have previously and instead allocate 30 minute study sessions with a short break of 10 minutes to do something nice in between.'

Here's the exercise that you can try for yourself. Start with the limiting statement you have associated with the desired behaviour change and then change the statement accordingly.

I want to… _____ **but**_____

I want to … _____ **but**_____

I want to…_____**and**_____**so**_____

I want to… _____**and**_____**so**_____

Examine what mood change occurs in you once you have done this. Discuss with a close friend how you hold this problem or behavioural change differently and make a note of what's just happened.

Begin with an end in mind…

Imagine many, many years from now you're attending the funeral of a close friend. As you enter the chapel, you begin to notice that there are several people there that you know. In fact this could be quite exciting now because the more you look around, the more you're surprised to notice that there are people there that you know and love too, just as much as your best friend!

As you approach the coffin to pay your respects, imagine the surprise you'd feel to see a picture on a frame of you mounted before the coffin. It suddenly becomes clear that this is in fact your own funeral.

Consider the kind of eulogy you'd want them to give from a point in the future, having made several changes if needed in your life. Have friends, acquaintances, business colleagues and loved ones come up and begin reading their eulogy of how they saw you and what you gave and how they helped them by your contributions to their lives.

Make a list here of 4 people and write brief notes about what they'd say about you at your own funeral. This is a reflection of how you have chosen to live too for the future.

Name and relationship	What they say in their eulogy to describe you in the future...

If you are currently living a life that feels out of control by the demands made upon you by many internal and external influences, a good way to get your feet firmly back on the ground is to stop and consider how in life you would like others close to you to remember you at your funeral.

I guarantee if you really think this through for a few minutes before doing this exercise you'll find none of them talking about the fact that you spent too much time worrying, working or stressing about things in the world. They'd prefer to remember you as a person who added something of value to their lives and this might act as a lynch pin for you to decide what are the really important things that matter most and help you put them ahead of the things that matter least but totally stress you and just allow you to survive in the human zoo as opposed to thriving in the future.

Session 7

Tips to Thrive in the Human Zoo

Researchers believe that we have between 40,000 and 60,000 thoughts each day and even if your concerns do come to become reality, around 80% of us will handle the realities and negatives better than we thought we would or could.

~**Negative thoughts are normal**. They're primarily there to protect you from harm. However, excessively running these in your mind becomes rumination and this may lead to increased anxiety. When rumination strikes, take time, to come up with alternative reframes about a situation. Being caught up in a mind boggling traffic jam is better than having been in the accident that caused it! Or getting cut up by another driver doesn't then mean you need to chase them down in your car, neither of you are going to the same place and neither of you need to be there at the same time!

~**Learned helplessness is a brain chemical reaction** Which is taking woes and regrets from the past and then mixing them with perceived threats from the future and bringing them into the present here and now, nothing more: 'A thought is just a thought and a feeling is just a feeling,' Tori Rodriguez (Psychotherapist in Scientific American). It's F.E.A.R. (False Evidence Appearing Real) like the Pike Syndrome experiment. Remember having watched the movie clip how he'd not only given up on eating the Minos but he'd also allowed himself not to even attempt to question the evidence and make the attempt to eat the Minos that were mere centimetres from his mouth? Dispute emotional thinking by using the A,B,C,D,E technique and maybe taking time to see the situation from the perspective of another person.

~**Consider attending mindfulness courses** or meditation programmes to work on remaining focused on the present, therefore avoiding regrets from the past and worries of the future. You could also practice future pacing positive outcomes in your life using self-hypnosis too. It's a fantastic tool - why not try this for yourself?

~**Write down your C.R.A.P. board list** and see how quickly brain dumping the stuff in your head onto paper calms you down.

~**Consider what good things came from going through a bad experience.** People who hone their ability to find benefit in situations have fewer, less disruptive thoughts, more meaning in their lives and are less likely to succumb to the propaganda of their monkey brain.

~**Think about doing the Putting First Things First Exercise** to check that what you're doing each and every day marries up to your real priorities as to how you would want to be remembered.

~**Acknowledge your thoughts and feelings,** don't suppress them. Name them specifically to reduce unconscious white noise. People who suppress their feelings tend to eat more comfort foods to cope with emotional overwhelm. There are no foods out there that actually taste better than feeling slim and energetic.

~**Avoid making comparisons between yourself and others**. This will help you overcome feelings of envy and guilt. Much of this comparison bias has been programmed into us by multi-national corporations that want us to buy their products and services in order to feel better. It's just shit brained thinking driven by a culture that fuels greed and the wants of the egotistical mind.

~**Avoid comparison to others where you work,** recall how feeling less empowered than your work colleagues will set you up to experience the tumult of hierarchical stress in the workplace and leave you feeling less satisfied with your occupation and workplace. Compare yourself alternatively to someone who is worse off than you might be right now. As I was writing this, the Olympic Athlete Oscar Pistorius was told that he wouldn't be released by South African authorities from his jail sentence, following the manslaughter of his former girlfriend, Reeva Steenkamp. I can't image how bad he might be feeling about the whole thing right now, having fallen completely from grace but chances are he'll be feeling a lot worse than most and there are a lot of people who are much worse off than you could ever imagine possible.

~**Set aside some time,** say 20 minutes, to worry in the day and keep to it. Remember to try some cardio activities shortly before doing so in order that your brain can be infused by happy chemicals first, which shift the act of worry to be something that you have to try to do rather than it coming over you like a black cloud.

~**Take a warm shower in the midst of your worry**. Warming yourself up and metaphorically washing away negatives down the drain can have a useful psychological impact on your demeanour very quickly too.

~**Become curious about other people**, this curiosity you express in others will increase their confidence and make you appear extremely charismatic. It will also help you keep out of your own head too. Additionally showing interest in others will cause them to reciprocate interest in you which can be incredibly good from an ego strengthening point of view.

~**Develop your awareness of social groups** to which others belong as you develop your charisma. This'll help you be a better judge of character of others, it will also increased rapport with others in your life and help you build a better understanding of the types of people you should spend your time with and those to avoid.

~**Embrace change more often,** the change will at first feel uncomfortable however, as you increase your experience of change, you will increase your own comfort zone which will make you less likely to succumb to the challenges of the fight or flight response when faced with new life changes.

~**List your strengths and weaknesses** as this will help you improve your understanding and knowledge of what things in life you excel at and what areas of your life require improvement. In the areas you need most help, ask someone for advice or an opinion on how you could make things better. Doing this will make you more likeable to the other person but will also encourage them to go out of their way to help you all the more.

~ **'Learn to say no before your body does'** is a phrase I've heard used by Dr Gabor Mate and he suggests that people who have a tendency to say yes, despite really wanting to say no to people, are often more prone to ill health and stress by having commitments they didn't want and certainly didn't ask for thrust on them. Saying 'No' doesn't make you a bad person, it makes you appear confident and in control of your life. This has to be smarter than if you're someone who is always struggling to meet the demands of others who offload their jobs on you. The act of saying 'No' isn't always easy for some people, so you can use any of the following phrases: 'You know I would love to do this to help you but I am unable to commit as I have other priorities requiring my attention at the moment.' Or, 'You know I would love to help out but now isn't a good time because I am in the middle of something, perhaps you could ask me again.' Or try my personal favourite, 'Thanks for asking me to help, I'd need to look at my schedule first before committing to do this. Let me come back to you if I happen to have time, I'd rather do that than agree and not be able to complete what I said I would.'

~**Prepare what you will do tomorrow, today!** Making a list of things that need your attention before completing work or going to bed is so useful as you can have time to sleep on this and allow your unconscious mind to process and organise your thinking in advance. This is a far better strategy than getting up out of bed and not having any real idea about what you want to achieve that day.

~**Procrastination breeds fear and is a stress inducer too.** Whatever you want doing tomorrow, try doing today and whatever you want to do today, why not do it now!

~ **Choose to do things in your life that mean you don't have to lie afterwards to cover your tracks**. A great deal of stress is caused when we lie to others or indeed ourselves.

~**Use mistakes as an opportunity to learn** from them and not berate yourself. You are never really as good or as bad as you tell yourself you might be. Dwelling on mistakes you make increases anxiety ten-fold and attempting to forget about them might mean you'll go ahead and make them all over again. Use mistakes in balance as an opportunity to review what went well, what went wrong and what might you do the next time round.

~**Perfect your ability to tolerate uncertainty**. Give up on this in yourself, others and how the world should be. The earth spins at around 1,650 kilometres an hour or 1,040mph and you want perfectionism? When you're continually being dogged by perfectionism you will be left feeling that things you do will never be good enough and this means that in time you seem to do less and reduce your efforts, which means you'll then spend more time lamenting what you should have done but didn't, what you could have become and didn't, much to the annoyance of those around you and more importantly to yourself. This strategy will leave you feeling stuck and forlorn.

~**Ensure you get enough sleep**. Sleep deprivation will cause you to see situations through a distorted lens, especially if you don't get to enjoy sufficient REM state sleep associated with rest, repair and healing. Stress also inhibits sleep as you find your thoughts continually interrupting your attempts to drift off.

There are several good strategies that can help you overcome insomnia including avoiding caffeine during the evening. Avoidance of excessive alcohol and stopping doing mentally demanding work before going to bed are old favourites. Remember it's easier to ride the wave of sleep when you do feel tired, so go to bed, don't try to overcome the sleep feeling as this is your brain telling you it needs rest and overriding this will mean that you'll increase your likelihood of insomnia later or struggle to actually go to sleep when you're not feeling tired and are in bed.

Other good approaches are to increase your body temperature before bed and have a bath which can often help you relax and prepare for sleep. Above all don't - and I can't stress this enough - use your tablet or smart phone in bed as the blue back light emissions from these electronic devices appears to scramble your naturally occurring circadian rhythms and rather like you'd do with an infant, aim to go to bed at the same times each evening so that your unconscious mind can become attuned to the predictability of your intentions around sleep.

Acknowledgements

I would like to thank several people especially my amazing wife Yumiko who first suggested that I write this book. Additionally to my beautiful daughter Ellie Jane who continued to encourage me with getting it done. Several other individuals deserve thanks too. Lucy Rahaman my administrator and Dionne Ward who regularly read draught after draught and helped no end make sure I kept the book interesting. I'd also like to extend great thanks to my fantastic psychotherapy friends Russell Potts and Steve Griffiths and his amazing wife Laura for their input and advice during the writing of this project and also I'd like to say a big thanks to the lovely boys and girls at my local Starbucks store in Shoreham who always welcomed me to spend time writing at their store making it my second office. Additionally I'd like to say a big thanks for the training offered to me with Uncommon Knowledge through Roger Elliott and Mark Tyrell who started me off on this great adventure back in 2000 you boys are off the scale amazing. Additional nods will also go to many of the great people who inspired the book through my studies over the years, additionally Dr Michael Coupland, my super friendly dental tutor who initially encouraged me to write a course for the NHS dental CPD programmes and always has a kind word to help bring me along. Peter Courtney Fitch also encouraged me to put my hand to this and has had a part to play and of course Tony, the coffee van man who served me, drinks most days and continued to remind me that I needed to get this done as well as my current author friends Simon Lelic and Sasha Stephens who were always happy to offer their guidance and help in running with this.

The illustrations and art work for this project were done by an amazing gentleman MCSKY 258 who is available on https://uk.fiverr.com/mcsky258 in case you need any illustrations done too. The formatting for this to Kindle was kindly done by a tremendous gentleman called Purger and you can get his help here https://uk.fiverr.com/purger1/format-your-kindle-book-perfectly

Suggested additional reading and information sources

Professor Robert Sapolsky -Why Zebras don't get ulcers

David Rock -Your brain at Work

Martin Selligman - Learned Optimism

Steve Peters - Chimp Paradox

Joe Elliott and Ivan Tyrell – Human Givens & The Origins of Dreams

Joseph Le Deux - The Emotional Brain

Women's Health Magazine November 2014 P128-129 Hoard Games

Flipnosis - Kevin Dutton

Frogs into Princes (The introduction to NLP)- Richard Bandler and John Grinder

Positive Personality Profiles - Robert A Rohm

Who do you think you are anyway? - Robert A Rohm

You've Got Style - Robert A Rohm

Man Watching- Desmond Morris

Yes! (50 Secrets from the science of persuasion- Robert Cialdini and Noah J.Goldstein

Emotional Intelligence Daniel Goleman

In the realm of Hungry Ghosts – Dr Gabor Mate

Printed in Great Britain
by Amazon